Undercurrent

A MEMOIR OF FEAR

Undercurrent

A MEMOIR OF FEAR

Leslie Volker

Mill City Press, Inc.
322 First Avenue N, 5th floor
Minneapolis, MN 55401
612.455.2293
www.millcitypublishing.com
undercurrent2015@gmail.com

ISBN-13: 978-1-63413-787-4
LCCN: 2015914673

Cover Design by Colleen Rollins

Printed in the United States of America

I would like to dedicate this book to Ed.

I know that without him in my life I would not be the person I am today.

Perception is an interesting word. Everyone's perception is different. I would like everyone who reads my book to understand that the stories I have written are from my perception, no one else's. Although characters in the stories may have a different perception, these are mine.

Acknowledgments

I would like to thank my parents and grandparents, along with all the other people in my life who have helped me grow into the person I am today.

I would also like to acknowledge the people who have helped me with this task of writing. I would like to thank my friend Jude for sticking with me and looking at the first draft and doing all the corrections of my terrible spelling and awful grammar. I would also like to thank Roxanne Sadousky for the two plus years of editing help and teaching me how to express myself with words. Last but not least Kay for doing the last edit of the entire book, again my grammar, spelling and sentence structure. I could not have done it without them.

PART I

It's Tuesday night and I walk into my first Al-Anon meeting. Ed has just gone into treatment for alcohol and I don't know what it means yet. I filed for divorce before Ed went into treatment But when he called me from treatment he said, "I want to come home, and I don't know how I feel about my religion right now. Would you hold off on the divorce while I figure it out?" For some reason, I said yes.

My stomach flutters. My fear starts knotted and painful in my stomach. My breath is tight and short and my heart pounds. I hear it. There are eight women sitting at a table in the church basement. I see Betty. She smiles at me and says, "Come sit next to me, I'm glad you're here." Betty's husband Gail and my husband Ed became friends after high school. We all drank together.

I am thirty years old, and for the first time in my life I think maybe things can change for the better. Until this moment, I didn't know I had choices, that I could change what is happening in my life.

After the meeting starts and the other women share their stories, I want to share mine but don't know how to start. I stammer. Betty says, "It's ok, I have been where you are and the meetings will help." I feel a little bit better. My heart slows down and I start to breathe normally again, but I'm still scared. As the other women talk, I try to figure out where my fear comes from. I have felt it all my life. Perhaps, these meetings will help me understand. I recall life in my childhood family and how those events and people formed who I am. I don't trust anyone and haven't for a long time.

I start going to Al-Anon every week. I am hopeful for the first time in years.

Who I Am

September 11,1943, Mom and Dad bring me home from Northwestern Hospital to our little house by Cedar Lake in Minneapolis. My birthday is September 4th. My mom got to pick the day because I was born by caesarean section. I don't know if it was an important date to her or just that she could have the surgery that day. My lungs didn't inflate, so they put me in an oxygen tent. Because of the c-section and my lungs, we stayed in the hospital for a about a week. There are four of us in my family: Mom, Dad, and my older sister Naomi. She is three and a half years old when I come home.

World War II has been going on for some time. Dad has left for the army. He is in the Special Services Entertainment Division because he plays the violin and can entertain the men. It's just Mom, Naomi and me. Grandma and Grandpa Supak, my mom's parents, live within walking distance, about a block and a half away. We spend a lot of time with them. When we are old enough to cross the street by ourselves, Mom says we can walk there anytime we want.

Sisters

I have funny, pointed eyebrows with ends that grow towards each other to make a point. My father has the same eyebrows and so does his mother. As I grow up I am very proud of them because I am the only grandchild who has them.

Our tiny home on a hill has chipped cement steps from the sidewalk to the path to our front door. There is a front porch and a little woods just on the other side of our small back yard. I live there until I am seven years old. My parents sleep in the sunroom, and Naomi and I share a bedroom. We have a small kitchen and a very dark basement. The basement has wooden steps with a railing that creaks and leads to a musty space filled with cobwebs and Mom's canned goods. I don't like going down there.

It's summer time and Mom takes us to Cedar Lake, which is small enough to see all the way around it. She stands me on the wood posts that hold the ropes for the swimming area, and I jump into the water. At nine months old I am fearless.

During nap time, I'd scoot my bottom to the end of the crib and put my legs straight up the end and sing the chorus of "Bell Bottom Trousers" word for word. I still remember the tune. I can't even talk. Sudie, our Japanese live in help, yells "Mrs. Ptashne, come see what your daughter is doing. I think we should take her to the radio stations and show her off." "Absolutely not," Mom says. Sudie is like part of our family, she takes care of Naomi and me and helps Mom with the house. When I am about one and a half or two years old Sudie goes away. I am too young to understand where she goes. It is not until I am much older that I understand why. Where is she? We never see her again. We never talk about it.

Dad has been home for some time and working for my Grandfather. He has brought home a television. I sit on the floor with my legs crossed, staring up at this brand new invention. It is a big old wood box with a screen no more than ten inches square. Naomi and I get up bright and early to watch test patterns. Test patterns come on before any shows start. They are a pattern of lines that are on the screen to let us know the TV is working but no shows are on yet. We are so excited to have this and we watch because that's all that's on at that time. At night we watch the Lone Ranger, Howdy Dowdy, and Milton Berle. Mom and Dad watch with us.

Sudie

I am five years old. It's a beautiful summer day and Naomi and I play outside. There are two Doberman pincers that live across the street from us that are always tied up, each with a muzzle. Mom has told us not to go near them. Suddenly, Naomi runs up the porch stairs. I turn my head and look. The two dogs are charging across the yard at me. Their leashes are dragging and torn behind them. Their muzzles are off and are flapping on the sides of their faces. They are barking and growling loudly. I run up the stairs and pull on the porch door but it is locked. "Let me in!" I scream at my sister, safe on the other side. I cry and pound on the door. She lets me in just as they are almost upon me. When I get in, I run crying to find my mother. I can tell Naomi doesn't like me. I'm not sure why, but she plays tricks on me like locking me out of the porch. Is this when my fear starts?

I ride in a freight elevator with Mom and Dad. It has a creaky slat wood door that has to be pulled up and down manually so the elevator can move. We are on our way to the top floor of the Wyman

5

Building in downtown Minneapolis. My grandfather's business is here. I run through the factory with all the sewing machines and people working. There is a wood floor and light fixtures hang from the ceiling by chains. In his office, he sits at a huge wood desk. I run to his chair, and he lifts me up and gives me a big hug.

I stand on a toilet seat as Mom dabs Calamine lotion on my chickenpox spots one by one. She is gentle and the lotion feels so good. I hope it stops the itching. A few days later, I hear Naomi screaming as she runs into the house. She was playing hide and seek with some friends in a vacant lot and a bee's nest fell on her. It is so awful. Mom takes Naomi into the bathroom to help her. She has red marks all over her body. I go to the door of the bathroom where she is with Mom, and she screams at me "Get out of here! I can't stand you!" I feel so sad as she slams the door in my face. Why doesn't she like me? What have I done?

I'm in first grade, and we take the city bus to school. I climb up the steps to board the bus. I wave at Mom because she walked me to the bus stop. Naomi is always with me, but not this time. I don't know where she is. Mom pinned tokens to my clothes so that I can take the bus home after school. At the end of the day I catch the bus home and climb those same steps. I go way to the back of the bus and sit on the long seat with black and green printed material that feels like velvet on my legs. My feet dangle because I can't touch the floor. I don't know where to get off because I'm alone. The bus ride seems very long compared to most days, and I'm scared, so I ride all the way to the bus garage. Tears are just inside my eyes the whole time. Our phone number is pinned inside my jacket or sweater and they call my mother to come get me. She is panicked and has been trying to find me because I didn't get off the bus at our spot. I am six years old. I am afraid of the city bus after that.

Mom tells me she loves to cook, and whatever she makes smells good. When friends come over I hear them tell her what a wonderful cook she is. The countertops in our kitchen are very crooked. On a bright, sunny afternoon I hear her yelling, "Oh! MY!" from the kitchen. I run in and what I see makes me start to giggle. Her beautiful golden brown pineapple upside down cake is upside down on the floor. It slid off the cooling rack. It truly is an upside down cake. We both start laughing so hard we can hardly stand up.

We are Jewish but don't go to the synagogue. It's Passover and my grandmother has set up the long table in her living room for all the people that are here. Some are relatives from New York that I don't know. But most are my aunts, uncles and cousins. My grandmother has been cooking all day. All the smells mingle together and it smells so wonderful. I wear my special yellow organdy dress with a big hoop skirt. For once I don't have on my cowboy boots and holster and Mom is happy. She tells me how nice I look. As I sit down on the couch, I forget to pull the hoop up from underneath me. It flies up and hits me in the face. My cousins start to laugh and make fun of me. It doesn't feel good. I don't like it but I don't say anything.

Mom and Grandma make all the special treats for all the Jewish holidays. Homantoshen, a cookie with three corners filled with a prune apricot jelly

Tomboy

Organdy dress

mixture for Purim. Carrot mold, a bread made in a Jell-O mold for Thanksgiving, and chicken soup with matzo balls for Passover. Beef brisket and popovers at Hanukah. I feel so loved when I eat these wonderful things. There is always food at our family gatherings. Whenever we go to Grandma's house there is food.

It's Sunday and we are at Grandma's house. We go every Sunday. The whole family is here--aunts, uncles, cousins and some friends. My little five-foot grandmother stands at the stove in her housedress making the most wonderful sour cream pancakes. She uses a curved pancake griddle on the gas burner. I watch her put lots and lots of butter on the griddle each time before the batter. She tells me, "The griddle is so seasoned that it is part of the taste." I'm not sure what that means but I don't care because they taste wonderful. She also makes enough batter to fill a mayonnaise jar for each family to take home for the week. When I'm older, I follow her around the kitchen to see if I can figure out how to make them. Her recipe starts with fourteen eggs. She says, "A pound of butter, maybe a little more, two cups of sugar, maybe a little less." When I make them, they don't taste as good, but I don't have her griddle. We stay all day and eat hamburgers with cold chicken at dinnertime. She always has chicken on Saturday night for dinner. We get the leftovers. I don't see anyone helping her. She just waits on us hand and foot. I don't see her ever sit down.

Grandpa is taking all eight of us cousins on an outing on a summer Sunday afternoon. I am the second to the youngest. He does this often when we are all together. We ride to Excelsior Amusement Park in Grandpa's Cadillac, singing at the top of our lungs, the car windows open, and the wind blowing my hair. My feet don't touch the floor. Excelsior is a great amusement park in Minnesota on Lake Minnetonka. I don't like the rides that go fast and up off the ground. I like the caterpillar and the Tilt-a-Whirl. We usually spend the whole day there. On the way there my cousin Judie turns around from the front seat and says. "Why are you singing? You don't have a voice!" I get very quiet. The fun is gone for me. I never sing with them again. I am seven or eight years old.

A voice is a box somewhere in our throats that helps us make sounds and words. One way to loose your voice is through cancer of the throat. They take your voice box out but you can still talk through a tube they put in your trachea. Another way you can lose your voice is if you believe everything others tell you, you might not feel worthy of speaking. I think this is what happens to me.

The Big House

I am seven years old and we move to a new house in St. Louis Park that I call the big house. It's a very modern home with a flat roof, lots of windows, a huge back yard and a big porch. I get to walk to school. Mom and Dad wanted a bigger house and knew the architect. As the story is told, Mom and Dad were having dinner one night at the architect's house, which he had built for himself. Dad said, "I love this house." Harley Johnson replied,"Great! You can buy it. I'll just build myself another one." He moved out and we moved in shortly after.

During these years my father works for my grandfather in his snowsuit factory, and our life is good. I have everything I ever wanted, but I am still afraid of everything.

We get out of the car in the garage. As we walk to the house, Dad says, "Stop," and he goes back in the garage to get a shovel. The walkway from the garage to the house is covered with black slimy lizards. The light from the street shines on them and they look scary to me. They are small but move quickly and climb all over each other to get out of there, but they aren't going anywhere. They have come from the swamp across the street from our house. There are a ton of them. Ick! Dad shovels them into the yard, and in the house we go. Now I don't like big dogs, I'm afraid of the bus, and really don't like the basement. I add lizards to the list.

I walk over to Judy's house less than a block away from mine. She has just moved into our neighborhood and we are in fourth grade. Her small house feels warm and cozy. I walk in without even knocking. I am happy. I spend as much time at her house as I do mine. Her family gives me the only nickname I ever had, Lestle. I drink so much Nestle's chocolate drink at their house they start calling me Lestle.

I run into the house yelling at my mom, "You gave me a boy's name, you gave me a boy's bike. What did you want? A boy!" They had given me my cousin Tom's little two-wheeler. It is tan and about three feet tall. Leslie is mainly a boy's name at that time, but mom named me after the actress Joan Leslie. The kids at school are teasing me about it. When Dad gets home, Mom says, "The kids are making fun of Leslie because of her bike." He takes me the next day to get my very own red three-speed girls bike. I am ecstatic. Now maybe the kids will stop teasing me.

Wonderful New Bike

Judy loves horses and we pretend we are riding. We name our bikes after horses. Her's is Fury mine is Red. We are always together and ride our bikes all over St. Louis Park with some other friends.

I am lying in front of the fireplace in my PJ's listening to music. My father and a few other musicians are playing string quartets. It's wintertime and the fireplace is lit and crackling. Lots of my parents' friends are over. As I have done many times before, I get up and go onto Forest Wiggins lap. I have known him most of my life. He is the only black man in the group. Mom has a big modern chair with wonderful big arms. It is called a Womb Chair,and when I sit in it, it feels like being swallowed in comfort. As we sit in that chair, Forest wraps his arms around me and I feel completely safe and loved. Then one day he doesn't come anymore. I miss him terribly. I never see him again. We don't talk about it, just like Sudie.

Mom always cooks her favorite blintzes for string quartet night. Rolled up dough with cooked cream cheese inside. Homemade strawberry jam on top. She cooks all day. The house smells wonderful, even though I don't like to eat them. Music flows through the house, out the windows and through the neighborhood. Just about the time dessert is served and music is still being played, I fall asleep on Forest's lap. He gently wakes me and says, "It is time to go to bed." The music drifts up to my bedroom as I fall asleep.

Everything is so sweet. Yet I wake up most mornings with a stomach ache and bite my fingernails down to the quick. I walk into Mom and Dad's bedroom and in a little voice say I don't want to go to school. I'm not sure why but my stomach hurts. Mom finally takes me to the doctor. I have to drink this icky, white chalky stuff for an X-ray. There is nothing physically wrong with me. They keep telling me I have to eat more ruffage.

It's Saturday morning and Mom has made me Cream of Wheat.

We are sitting in the kitchen at the table together listening to "Let's Pretend" on the radio. The show was broadcast with an audience full of children beginning with Uncle Bill Adams' salutation, "Hello Pretenders!" followed by the response "Hello, Uncle Bill!" After some back and forth with the kids, the show would launch into an adaptation of classic childrens stories and fairy tales like Rumpelstiltskin, Sleeping Beauty, Thumbelina and many, many more. After we are done, I go into the den. The TV and stereo are built into a little cubby hole and I sit on the floor listening to the records of Cinderella while turning the pages of the book, over and over and over. It is my favorite story. I pretend that I am Cinderella, and that someday my prince will come and get me.

Naomi and I are begging and begging to have a Christmas tree. We want to be like everyone else. There are trees and decorations all over our school. My mother gives in; she always gives in. She puts blue and white lights on the bushes in front of the house and gets us a tree! She decorates it with little flags from all over the world. We beg for stockings to be hung on the fireplace. Wow! What a morning this is. It's Christmas morning 1951. We have never celebrated this before. We run downstairs and grab the stockings off the fireplace and find oranges, apples and those little cars that, if you rub them on the floor, they take off and zoom really fast. It is such an exciting day. That night we light the candles on the Menorah for Hanukah.

I am ten years old at summer camp. It is Camp Fire Girls by Lake Minnetonka. I don't like it. I don't like sleeping away from home. After we moved to the big house, I went to stay overnight at a neighbor's house from the old neighborhood, and I got sick and threw up. Mom had to come get me at two in the morning. I just want to be in my own bed and cover up with my own blankets.

A friend that I met at camp and I are sitting at dinner and we switch our food. I love meat loaf and she doesn't. I hate salad and she loves it. The counselor sees us and gets us each another serving. The counselor says, "You will sit here until this is gone." We have been sitting here such a long time it feels like hours. We are in uncomfortable folding chairs. I get more and more angry but don't say anything. I eat the salad but gag on every bite. The next year, when it is time to sign up for camp, I tell my mother she has to write a letter telling them I don't eat salad or I won't go. Mom won't write the letter. "You have to learn to eat new things," she says. Mom makes spaghetti and meatballs, and I don't let the sauce touch the noodles and sometimes have no sauce at all. She and my grandmother always go downtown to Dayton's Department store and bring home Eclairs. I don't eat them because the ingredients touch. When I'm older, I think of all the wonderful eclairs I missed out on. I go to camp the next year but start getting bloody noses everyday. No one knows why. They finally call my mom to take me to the doctor. My nose needs to be cauterized. I don't go back to camp ever again.

There is something going on that I don't understand. I think it is about politics and I keep hearing the name Joe McCarthy and Communism. There is a lot of whispering when my parents' friends are over. Some are standing up and some are sitting. They are all talking fast. Their foreheads are wrinkled up like they are worried about something. Some also look angry and their voices are raised. I think it is about politics because everything changes when they talk about politics.

Who are Mom and Dad?

Mom   Dad

Grandma loves to tell the story of how Mom was born in Russia, a country that seems dark and scary from the stories she tells.

Mom's name is Ida Supak and she was born on April 4, 1912, in Berdichev, Russia. She came to this country with my grandmother when she was two years old. They lived on the north side of Minneapolis. Most of the Jewish people lived in the same area. She went to a Yiddish school for a short time until it closed. There weren't enough teachers to keep it going. She attended North High for high school. She loved to sing and sang in all the operas and musicals for the four years. The story is that she went to Juilliard School of Music in New York, where she met my father.

Mom stays home and takes care of us even though she was told by Dimitri Metropolis, the conductor of the Minneapolis Symphony at the time, that she had a voice that should be given to the world. She should not have children and should just sing. She was pregnant with my sister and didn't feel she could do both.

She is about 5 foot 2 inches and has blond hair. I think she is beautiful. Mom goes to the beauty shop and has her hair colored to make it brighter. She has fair skin and wonderful hazel eyes. I have heard her say she is heavy, and she reminds us all the time not to eat too much so we don't get fat. I don't know what fat means because she looks fine to me. When I am two years old, she gets diabetes. These two things set up a pattern in our house. She always watches what we eat, and she always cooks a balanced dinner. Meat, salad, vegetable and some kind of dessert. I don't like salad and I don't like vegetables. I hardly eat anything. When I am older and married with kids, I put vegetables on the table every night and usually end up throwing it away because my family doesn't eat them either.

Mom, in a pair of my father's boxer shorts and a little elastic top that has bare shoulders, is out in our back yard to work in the flower gardens. She loves to be outside. She puts on a pair of gardening gloves and works and works. Everything she touches turns out well. The gardens have wonderful flowers. There are white, purple and yellow irises in the front and daisys, begonias, and many more I can't remember in the back yard. I always smell the flowers in the house. There are also tomatoes and cucumbers. She is lying out in the sun today on a lawn chair in the same outfit. I go out and sit on the ground next to her. "I love the sun. It makes me feel so wonderful," she says. She doesn't tan very well but she loves it. I feel the same way. The sun is so warm on my skin, and I feel healthy and strong.

When her diabetes is out of control because she needs something to eat or doesn't have enough insulin, she screams a lot. She becomes a different person. "Why are you late? You know I have to eat on time!" she would rage whenever my dad walked in five minutes late from work. We wait for dad to get home because she does not eat or serve dinner until he is. "Go wash up so we can eat!" she would yell in Yiddish. They always speak Yiddish when they don't want us to know what they are talking about. Dad rushes to get ready for dinner. Mom's rage gets us all to the table quickly. I feel my stomach tighten again at dinner but don't know what to do about it. On nights when Dad gets home early, things are calm. Dad lies down on the couch for ten minutes or so. He is refreshed and funny at dinner. There is more conversation and my stomach is not tight.

I hear Mom talking to friends and to my dad that she doesn't know how to take care of her diabetes. The doctors tell her, "Go home and take care of yourself." She feels ashamed. Mom has so many different moods. Sometimes she's screaming and angry. Most of the time with me she is loving and kind. She always makes sure I am all right. Breakfast is fixed, lunch is prepared, and there are always good dinners. Although those are things all parents should do, I hear some don't. But not Mom. It seems I always come first and have a strong feeling of love for her.

Mom taught me things I remember all my life: how to put on make-up--always understated, how to dress--always matching, no white until after Memorial Day, and white always goes away Labor Day weekend, and how to entertain--always have enough food and a great looking table. I also learn about love.

My father's given name is Isadore Ptashne. He was born on May 19, 1909 in Chicago, Ill. He is a very good-looking man. He has dark black wavy hair, is about five foot ten inches tall, and has the brightest smile I have ever seem. His eyes sparkle when he laughs. He started playing the violin when he was fourteen, and it became his dream. He tells us that his parents didn't have a lot of money, but his sister Lottie paid for his lessons. Lottie is four years older and has been working for several years to help with the bills for my grandparents. She also decides when Dad is sixteen that she doesn't like the name Isadore, so she changes it to Theodore. I'm not sure how she does that and Dad doesn't explain. He also has two younger brothers.

We drive to Chicago every summer to see Aunt Lottie and the rest of Dad's family who still live there. Dad's younger brother, who has lived in Minneapolis for a few years, and his family are in another car. We stick together the whole way.

My grandparents, Dad's parents, live in the back of the dry cleaning shop they own. It is small but cozy. Grandpa Max gives my cousin Phyllis and me each a nickel to go to the corner store to get some candy. We get plastic lips, little plastic pop bottles, six to a pack, with some sort of liquid in them that tastes really sweet, bubble gum cigars, and button candy. We come back with a bag full. Phyllis lives in Chicago. She is a year older, and I am really glad to see her. We get along great even though we only see each other a couple of times a year.

We stay in a hotel down by the lake. If we take the underpass we can get to the beach without going outside. Phyllis stays with us at the hotel. We see my grandparents every day. My Grandma Rose has a beautiful head of white hair and eyebrows like mine. Dad tells us she has had a full head of white hair since she was twenty-one years old. Grandpa has pitch-black wavy hair. I don't know them well, but they are loving. When they see us, they are smiling really big smiles. They run to our car and hug us great big bear hugs. I can tell they are glad to see all of us.

My father has a gentle soul, I can tell, but he tells a story revealing a different side from when he was younger. He was a taxi driver to earn money while going to college and once got mad at a fellow driver. He threw a wrench at him and broke his leg. I think he is afraid of something like that happening again, because we are not allowed to get angry. The rules in our house are: you never hang up the telephone on anyone, you never slam the door in anyone's face, and you never lie. Sometimes I see a controlled anger on Dad's face if we don't follow the rules. But he'll just say, "Go to your room," and we know he is angry about something we did. Sometimes I feel angry but I don't know what to do with it.

Dad loves everything about music. I can tell he loves us kids, but I think he loves music more. Mom and Dad met in New York while Mom was at Juilliard School of Music, and dad was studying violin and working. They come back to Minneapolis in 1940 because he is offered a job in the Minneapolis Symphony as a violinist. It is only a thirty-two week season. He doesn't make enough money to support us, so he only stays a few years. He goes to work for my grandfather as a salesman.

Grandma and Grandpa Supak

Grandpa and Grandma

My grandparents are a very important part of my life. I want to know more about them now that I am older, I want to know more about their history. My cousin Paul did an interview with our grandmother and put together the story of their escape from Russia. Listening to the six cassette tapes he gave me helps me understand and respect them even more then I already do.

My Grandpa Supak was born Enoch, (the English translation was Henry Supak), in Berdiehev, Russia on July 2, 1886. This date is up for grabs because he used a Jewish lunar calendar, so the date may either be the first or the second of July. He liked to say he was born on the Fourth of July, his rebirth into this new nation.

He was raised with his sisters and brothers in an Orthodox Jewish home.

In Russia at that time, men were required to go into the army for seven years. Jews were not treated well, and he had been taught by his family that violence was not the way to settle things. He had met my grandmother, and they decided to get married because married men after the age of nineteen were exempt. They married in 1906. My grandfather was twenty and my grandmother was sixteen. He was drafted anyway. I don't know why. Maybe it was because he was a Jew and they didn't care about the rules when it came to Jews.

He entered the Czar's army but soon was writing my grandmother about the hard life and harsh treatment of Jews and other minorities. They were made to work harder with less food then the others. The Christians didn't like the Jews, but needed them for the work details. Grandpa said he had to get out. It was 1907. He asked her to meet him in a particular spot along the army camp fence where he would be that night on patrol. He asked her to bring a change of clothes. She tossed the clothing bundle over the fence, after he changed he carefully folded his uniform laid his gun on top of his uniform with a note saying, "This is the uniform of Enoch Supak." He felt if he did that, they would know he had escaped and not blame anyone else for his actions. He did not want any other person blamed because they couldn't identify whose uniform was left at the fence. He climbed over the fence and was gone. He thought it might help his fellow soldiers, but the authorities could do whatever they wanted and accuse anyone, even though the uniform was there. He never knew if they did or not.

They traveled incognito and ended up in a small town on the eastern coast of Crimea overlooking the Black Sea, where they settled for four years. Grandpa got a job as a shoe designer for a small company as that was his trade, and soon he was made the manager. He was very well liked and respected. They liked this town and wanted to stay but there was a jealous man who worked at the shoe company with my grandfather. He was jealous because my grandfather was so well liked and promoted quickly. This man knew their story. He turned my grandfather in as a deserter. The constable came to arrest him personally. Because he admired my grandfather so much he made sure he was treated well. They could have arrested my grandmother as an accomplice, but didn't.

After my grandfather's arrest, my grandmother sold a few things that they had and went back to her parent's house in Berdiehev. One of the stories she shared on the tapes, was being in jail on a false charge. She told us she had her first child Rose and was pregnant with my mother. Waiting at night for the knock on the door, they all feared that the police could take them away for just about anything they wanted to trump up. When it finally came, they took her away and tossed her in jail, where she was for four months. A new jailer or magistrate finally sent for her. He asked, "Did you do this?" She had no idea what "this" was. But knew her only chance of getting out was to lie. She said she had no knowledge of her husband's business, that he had abandoned her, and that she wasn't involved. The jailer let her go. By the time she was done with that story my stomach was tied in knots from sadness.

When she got back to her parent's house after being in jail for the four months, she found out Rose had died. They said Rose, who was two years old, was pulled off the bed by a dog. My grandmother always hated dogs. Now she realized she had to focus on the child that was about to come. On the night my grandmother went into labor, the mid-wife was not available. She ran through deep muddy roads to get home from work to her parents house. My mother was born that night.

My grandfather escaped from his jailers. He had been sentenced to five years of hard labor and he was being taken to a labor camp. They made a stop in Odessa where my grandfather had been for a short time. He asked the guard to let him go to the saloon to say good-bye to friends. They went together. After the guard had many shots of vodka, he passed out. My grandfather walked out of the saloon and headed east to find my grandmother. My grandmother told us in the tapes that she never told my grandfather she had been jailed.

After he found my grandmother back in their little town in Russia, he went on ahead to Hungary to work and save enough money to send for her. She stayed with her parents while she waited.

A story we heard all the time growing up was how my grandmother left Russia for Hungary with my mother. When my mother was six weeks old, my grandmother got a letter from my grandfather that it was time to leave. She was to meet with a guide at a certain checkpoint to escape. There was still great tension from the Russian authorities to get all the Jews out of the country. There were attacks called Pogroms on Jewish homes and shops by Russian guards everywhere in Russia. In the pre-dawn hours she and a small group were taken to a place where they had to hide in the reeds in a row-boat until guards passed. The man who had the boat told my grandmother that if the baby made a sound he would dump them overboard. My grandmother held my mother so tightly that she was not breathing when they got to the other side. They put her in cold and hot water to bring her back.

I don't have any other details of that escape. I just know my grandmother and mother were in Hungary for two years. My grandfather came to the U.S. through Galveston, Texas, on a special program for skilled Jewish workers. He was sent to Minnesota because the weather was similar to his Russian birthplace. He worked hard so he could send for his family. It took those two years.

All through this time that he worked to save money and bring his family to America he was very politically active, as he would remain all his life. As a true humanitarian who believed in freedom for all people, he lived what he spoke. When he came to Minnesota the only way he could follow through with his beliefs was through politics. He was a very liberal man but not a very religious man.

For a few years after he came here he worked in his trade as a shoemaker. He and a friend started a business as peddlers going door-to-door selling wares. I'm not sure what they sold. He did this until he found out the man was cheating him. He and my grandmother had a restaurant for a short time also. Later he started his own business. It was called Supak and Son. He had one son. The brand was Weather Winky. His business was a snowsuit manufacturing company during the late 1940's and 1950's. My aunt designed the first one-piece snowsuit for babies. There was a small white plastic winking snowman attached to the zipper on every snowsuit.

When I am older he tells me, "I pay and treat my employees well because I don't like the control unions have over them." He adds, "I want my employees to be free to make choices on their own." Freedom was the most important thing for our family. Although politics and religion are not the paths I've taken, I believe as they did about freedom. All my uncles and my father worked for him. They were all accepted without question. After all the uncles joined the company he changed the name from Supak and Son to Supak and Sons. He treated the uncles like sons.

He is not a tall man, maybe five foot nine, with a bald spot on the top of his head glasses, and a paunch of a stomach--not fat, just round. He smokes a pipe that smells like cherry. I love it.

He is accused of being a Communist in the McCarthy era.

Politically he is a member of the Progressive Party.

The Progress Party is an independent political party formed in 1948. The party supports Wallace/Taylor for President. Their platform supports the end of segregation, full voting rights for blacks and universal government health insurance.

In 1948 my grandparents, parents, my aunts and uncles, and their friends are working to get Henry Wallace elected. We go to many picnics and political meetings with speakers. They are all accused of being Communist. This includes my grandmother and my parents. The McCarthy era hits them hard. Friends are questioned about the family politics, all because they believe in freedom. I ask Judy to go to a picnic with me. Her dad says she can't go and I don't understand. We spend so much time together and he won't let her go. I go home and ask Mom why. She says, "It's a political picnic for the Progressive Party and some people think it's Communist even though it's not." I don't understand because I just want to go and have fun and play tag and run around with Judy and my cousins.

It's early 1980's. My nephew has done research and gotten the FBI files on my parents and grandparents. I ask him to send me a copy. I am sitting here reading the four hundred pages that they have collected on my family. It is surreal. After reading the files it feels like politics and being Jewish are synonymous. I can feel the fear they must have felt. Most of the pages are redacted and some of the stories are outlandish. It actually says, "Mr. Supak (my grandfather) donated money to the Progressive Party. We need to get some of that Jew money." Amazing. They also said, "The Ptashne's have one daughter and one son named Leslie." They didn't even know who we were.

My cousin Paul gives me a lot of information. There is a story he tells about the FBI coming to visit my grandparents' home. He thought it was 1963 or 1964. Two men got out of the car, walked across the lawn, and rang the doorbell. Grandma told Paul she went down the steps to open the door and one of the men asked , "Is Mr. Supak home?" She said, "Pa, do you want to talk to the FBI?" He simply says, "No." He was standing on the landing where they could see him. She turned to the men and said, "My husband doesn't want to talk to you." They turned around and walked back to their car without one more word. Paul can still hear Grandma's joyous laugher.

What is McCarthyism

What was McCarthyism? The dictionary describes McCarthyism this way:

1. The practice of making accusations of disloyalty, especially of pro-Communist activity, in many instances unsupported by proof or based on slight, doubtful, or irrelevant evidence.
2. The practice of making unfair allegations or using unfair investigative techniques, especially in order to restrict dissent or political criticism.

Joe McCarthy was a Senator from Wisconsin who took a stance against liberal people. He worked with the FBI to accuse many of being Communist. During the McCarthy era, thousands of Americans were accused of being Communist or Communist sympathizers. Primary targets were government employees, entertainers and others in the entertainment industry, educators and union activists. Many Jewish people were on the list. They were called before The House Committee on Un-American Activities, commonly referred to as HUAC.

This committee soon began to subpoena screenwriters, directors and other movie industry professionals to testify. The sixty-four thousand dollar question, as it became known, was "Are you now or have you ever been a member of the Communist Party of the United

States?" They were also asked to name names of people they knew who were members of the Communist Party.

Among the many that were called before the committee, the most famous group were ten men from the movie industry. They were called before the Committee and decided not to cooperate. They became known as the "Hollywood Ten". I have a signed copy of the book called Hollywood on Trial by Gordon Kahn, signed to my parents by Dalton Trumbo, one of the men accused. "To Ted and Ida with thanks and affection." These men citied the first amendment of free speech and free assembly, which they believed would protect them from prosecution, but it didn't work. They were all sentenced for contempt of court. Two of the men were sentenced to six months in jail and the rest to one year.

On November 25, 1947, the president of the Motion Picture Association of America announced the firing of the Hollywood Ten and stated, "We will not knowingly employ a Communist or a member of any party or group which advocates the overthrow of the government of the United States." They had never admitted to being Communist. This became known as the Hollywood Blacklist.

I think there were two reasons why the Jewish people were accused more than others. One reason was because at that time most Jewish people were liberal. The second was that most had come to this country from Russia. The government was afraid of Communism taking over the country. It was the time of the Cold War with Russia. Joe McCarthy took the position that all liberal and Russian immigrants were Communist. The government believed him.

Future witnesses who decided not to cooperate pleaded the Fifth Amendment protection against self-incrimination. Although this did protect them from prison, many were fired from their jobs. Once fired from jobs under these circumstances, they could no longer get work anywhere else.

I learned while researching that our friend Forest Wiggins was a professor at the University of Minnesota and fired from his job on the grounds that he had not published anything, but he actually had. He was a member of the Progressive Party, liberal, and black. All the criteria for being accused of being a Communist. At that time if you were fired from a teaching position, you could never get another job in Minnesota. He moved back to South Carolina. That is why we never saw him again.

It also became clear that Hollywood would not survive without these men. Many worked under ghost names to produce, direct and write for movies over the next few years while the blacklist was still in effect.

No wonder I don't like politics or want anything to do with it. How did something like this happen?

Grandma Supak was born Shrifa Katz, the English translation is Sophie, on August 25, 1890, in a small town outside of Berdichev, Russia. She also comes from an Orthodox Jewish family and started working at the age of ten to help support her parents, brothers and sisters. For a short time, she was a seamstress, but not paid. Seamstresses had to do an apprenticeship for several years before getting paid. She worked with an older girl who took her under her wing. The older girl was involved in the socialist movement and got her involved. She finally got paid while working at a chair-making factory. These chairs were called bentwood chairs because the wood was bent into a round shape molded for the back. Bentwood chairs are still made today. The women in the factory soaked the dowels in caustic chemicals that softened them enough to bend. She was the oldest girl in her family, and had a great deal of responsibilities. She was used to working hard by the time she came to the United States.

She learned to read and write with other children in secret gatherings at night. The group of women who taught the girls were known as "the young socialists". At age nine, she joined the girls in an effort to organize the maids who worked for the wealthy Russians. My grandmother had an early and humanistic start in politics. They all believed the same way and started going to secret meetings about the politics in Russia. She mets my grandfather at one of the meetings. She was fourteen years old. Although she was very shy, she learned very quickly and had very strong opinions about what she believed.

My grandmother came into this country through Canada. In Minnesota she was very active politically. She attended meetings called "The Women's Circle", where all the women got together to talk politics. There were other meetings held by the Progressive Party at several locations around the Twin Cities. She was accused of being a Communist in the years that Joe McCarthy was in office.

It is a politically scary time for my parents and grandparents. I know this because I hear them talking. I remember when I was about six or seven years old we went to a convention in Chicago and I stood up on a chair to see what was going on. Dad told me a man named Paul Robison was speaking. Later after we are back home I hear him say, "The FBI is following us." Dad says, "I saw a friend on the street today,and when he saw me, he crossed to the other side so he wouldn't have to talk to me."

As I grow up I learn that it was the time when Senator Joe McCarthy was at the height of his witch hunt of liberal people. My family and some of their friends were accused of being Communist. A vast majority of the people accused are Jewish. By 1951, the Federal Bureau of Investigation (FBI) has started files on most everyone accused. The FBI watches where my parents and grandparents go and who they talk to. The FBI even checks the mailboxes to see what mail they get. I'm still not sure what it all means, but I can tell everyone is scared. Dad is still gone a lot of nights playing his violin, and Mom still has friends over, but they go to a lot of meetings with my grandparents. Sometimes we go along when the meetings are at my grandparents house. I usually just watch TV or play with my cousins if they are there also.

For a short time we go to Jewish Sunday school. It is an old house on Park Avenue with a long wooden staircase. All us kids are running up and down. We're sitting on the floor listening to music, and singing "It's a Small World After All". All the friends and family that I know are here. I realize it's a school for all the kids whose parents feel about religion as my parents do. We are learning history and heritage, not religion. After about a year we don't go anymore because people are afraid

I think about and wonder what their fear feels like. Is it the same as mine? I never ask them.

Then I Go To Junior High

I'm thirteen now and belong to Bnai Brith Girls (BBG). The boys we hang around with are in Aleph Zadik Aleph (AZA) Jewish youth groups. We go to a lot of Bar and Bat Mitzvahs. We spend Saturday mornings at the Synagogue listening to our friends recite from the Torah. I don't understand any of the Hebrew language and I feel out of place. Because my family doesn't go to the synagogue, this is unfamiliar territory. I feel like everyone is staring. I'm very self-conscious. Sometimes I go with Judy and her family to Friday night services. I still feel out of place. I always want my parents to go with me. When I ask them if we can join, they say no. I go with Judy and her family a few more times but it still doesn't feel right. If I am Jewish and hang around with all the Jewish kids, then why don't we belong to the synagogue?

I ask my parents why we don't go, and they say, "You don't have to go to a synagogue to be a good Jew." I just accept that, and I stop going with Judy.

Naomi and I don't have much to do with each other. She hangs out with her friends and has a part time job after school. One day when Mom isn't home, Naomi calls, "Come here. I have something to show you." We have a big walk-in closet where Mom stores all her out of season clothes and bathroom supplies. Naomi says, "Take a very big sniff of this. It really smells good." I take that big sniff, my eyes water, and I can hardly breath. My heart starts pounding; I almost pass out. It is ammonia! She laughs and walks away. Why doesn't she like me?

It's the start of seventh grade. A new high school is being built so we go to school in split shifts. Naomi goes in the morning, and I go from 12:00-5:00. It's kind of nice.

I have on one of her good sweaters. I know if she catches me, I'll be in big trouble. I take it off and put it away before she gets home from work. In her drawer, I see her diary. I try to get it open but break the lock as I try. I am sitting on the bed reading what she has written. I don't understand much of what it says. There is stuff in there about her boyfriend and school and work, but nothing about me. I just put it away knowing she is going to kill me for sure when she sees what I have done. I am really scared. When she comes home from work she finds the diary. She knows I have read what she has written. She screams at me how much she hates me. I cower. I don't know if my mom can hear her, or if she ever tells my parents. She also knows I have taken her clothes but can't prove it. I lie the biggest lie I have ever told. I tell her, "I didn't touch any of your stuff." I am a brat, a younger sister that she hates. I still don't know why, so I lie. I just want her to like me. Do I do these things to get back at her for the way she treats me? Do I want her to hurt just like I do? I don't know.

It's summer time again and a very nice warm day. I am dressed in Bermuda shorts and a blouse. I have very long hair that my mother won't let me cut. She loves my long hair and puts it in pigtails on either side of my head. They hang down to my shoulders. I'm cutting through an alley on my way to a friend's house. At the end of the alley, a very large Great Dane charges at me. He jumps up and puts his paws on my shoulders. I turn my head away and wait for the bite. It never comes. He starts licking me all over my face. I push him down and run the rest of the way to my friend's house. I go a different way home and never cut through an alley again.

I have just gotten out of the shower and call Mom to comb my hair. I can't get all the snarls out myself after washing it because it is so long. I am thirteen years old. She yells back at me, "Not now." I sit at the top of the stairs in the big house, listening to a conversation between another man and woman whose voices I don't recognize. I start to cry because everyone is so angry. Naomi tells them she is married and having a baby. It is 1956 and she is sixteen years old. My parents are devastated. My mother is crying and my dad sounds sad. There is a catch in his throat when he talks. I feel sorry for all of them, even though I don't completely understand what is happening. What is the big deal? How exciting a baby is! My first niece or nephew. After the baby is born, I take pictures of him to school, but none of my friends seem interested. I can't figure out why. Years later when I have lunch with Judy's mom Reva, and we talk about my childhood, she understands because she was so much a part of it. She tells me about a day when Judy came home from school really angry at the kids at school. She tells me, "The kids were scoffing at you because of Naomi and it made Judy really angry."

Even with this happening, I have a wonderful time in seventh grade. Except for the studying part. My parents say to me, "Go up stairs and study," but I don't know what to do. So I talk on the telephone and listen to the radio and I don't do my homework. I am not a good student. I want to take French but the school won't let me because my English isn't good enough. I am almost failing all my classes, including gym.

I have two groups of friends. The ones from grade school and new friends I have met that came to junior high from different schools. We don't hang out together which seems funny to me since were all

Jewish. It's a summer night before we start eighth grade, and one of my grade school friends calls, "Come on over. Some of the girls are here." I walk into the porch and several other grade school girls are sitting in a circle. She says, "We have talked. Either you go around with us all the time or you don't go around with us at all." Without saying a word, I just turn around and walk out. As I walk the short six blocks home, the tears are running down my face and I decide to never, and I mean *never*, speak to them again, not one of them in either group. When I get home and tell Mom what happened, she tries to help. She says, "They are all crazy. Ignore them." I don't listen because deep down I think I have done something wrong, but I don't know what it is. Why can't we all be friends? I really don't understand. On the first day of school, I am scared and angry when I wake up. I don't want to go. I put on my new black and white checked dress with my black patent leather Capizios and comb my hair. My stomach tightens as I walk to the bus stop. I don't want to be there and I don't know what to do. I'm thinking, "What if I see them? What if I run into them? Will I throw up?"

I see one of the gals coming down the hall. As she gets closer, I look away. She doesn't say anything. I do the same with each of the girls. I cut myself off from the only friends I have ever known. I don't even talk to Judy. I have met a few non-Jewish girls but never feel like I fit in. I feel like I don't belong anywhere. I blame them. It is their fault I am unhappy. I am alone.

I started ballet lessons when I was five. I remember when I was five and walked into the ballet studio for the first time. It had wonderful shiny wood floors, ballet bars on each side of the room and mirrors behind the bars. I loved to dance. I took lessons every week until I was thirteen. When I start to develop, I won't put on the leotards anymore. I am self-conscious because I am gaining weight. I haven't noticed my body before. Now it is all I notice.

I am fifteen and up in my bedroom trying to fall asleep. I'm awake because even at fifteen I don't like to be home alone and I'm scared. My parents come home from an evening out. They are fighting. My mother is yelling at my father, "Remember the time you wanted to leave and take Naomi and not Leslie." That is all I hear. I pull the covers up over my head and cry myself to sleep. The amazing thing about this is that instead of getting mad at my father for not wanting me, I get mad at my mother for yelling at my father. I come downstairs the next morning mad, snotty, sarcastic and mean. She never knows what has hit her. We don't talk about it. Why have I pushed away the only person in my life I feel secure with? I know I love her more then just about anyone. She has always been there for me. Making Cream of Wheat when I'm sick, sitting with me to listen to Lets Pretend, just spending time with me and being there for me. We don't talk a lot, no one in my family does, but I just know she loves me.

I must know somewhere deep inside that no matter how I treat Mom, she will not go away. I'm not sure about Dad. I don't trust him anymore. What if he left, would he want me?. Since we are not allowed to get mad, how can I get mad at him? And as much as I love him, he isn't around much. He works during the day and plays his violin a lot of nights. He is also the disciplinarian. If we do something wrong, he is the one who punishes us, usually sending us to our rooms. He is also the funny one. When we are all together on good nights he makes me laugh, and I know I love him very much. I just don't have any idea what to do about all the feelings I have or how to talk about what is happening in our house or with my friends.

Naomi and Jim have bought a house in New Hope. Jim isn't Jewish and we started to celebrate Christmas with the whole family at their house. My grandparents are here, as are my cousins and their families. We have dinner and open presents. Naomi even has a tree.

I love Christmas. It is fun, but still very confusing. I know we do this to be with Naomi and her children, but what about our traditions? Again, my parents never talk about it. We are Jewish. Why do we now celebrate Christmas just to be with Naomi? Hanukkah goes away. Hence the confusion.

Naomi is driving me home from babysitting. I babysit a lot. Seems like most weekends. A friend of theirs is along, so Jim can stay with the kids. A car has come out of nowhere and broadsides us. Naomi jumps out of the car screaming, "Help us!" and jumps over a six foot fence. How did she do that? I am not hurt but crying and sitting on the curb. My knee is bleeding, but I don't feel anything. I'm not sure how I got out of the car. The police come. They ask Naomi how to get ahold of our parents. After they tell Dad what has happened, he tells the police to tell Naomi, "Get in and drive to the hospital or you may never drive again." Because she is so frightened, he says this will help her get over the fear of driving. Naomi's friend has a shattered wrist. I don't want to babysit after that.

Life Changes

My grandfather has retired. My uncle Nate, my mother's brother, has taken the Snowsuit Factory to North Carolina because labor is cheap there. He doesn't want my dad and my other uncles who work for him to go along. They are all out of work. Dad has worked for Grandpa ever since he left the orchestra. I am now fifteen and don't know anything different. Dad and his brother Fred buy a candy factory. They have the most wonderful little cakes called petits fours. Little cakes about an inch square with layers and layers of cake and frosting. I see vats and vats of chocolate when I visit Dad at work. I can even tell by the design on top of each piece what kind of candy it is. They can't sell them. I hear Dad talking to Mom, "I was at Dayton's today and they aren't interested." The business goes bankrupt. I am sixteen. I think it has only been a year since he started the business. I have always had whatever I want, and now we have nothing. No money, no food, we lose everything except the house. Dad and I are standing in the carport. The men come to take the car away. They drive off with my dad's favorite car. I am so sad watching them. I feel how my dad feels. There are no tears but the sadness is overwhelming, even for me. My mother and father are fighting all the time. My grandfather helps pay for what we need, including food. My father is ashamed and embarrassed.

Nate is the only boy on my mother's side of the family and the youngest. When Nate took the business away, he changed my family.

With all the anger in the house already from the diabetes and Dad working so much and not being around much, I'm not sure what to do. It adds to all the other feelings of confusion I am having and still not sure what to do with.

At age sixteen I am quiet and holding everything in. I wonder what is happening around me, but I don't ask questions. I never ask questions. I'm not sure I know what to ask, or if my parents will tell me. They are so protective of me ever since Naomi got pregnant and married. Yet, with Naomi out of the house I feel completely alone. I like that she doesn't live with us any longer, but now Mom and Dad are yelling at each other all the time. I go to my room and play the radio very loud. If I can't hear, maybe it isn't happening. I feel so much confusion with all these things happening to me. I'm feeling fat, I don't think I have any real friends, and there is anger all around me. I don't trust anyone. I walked away from my friends, but I can't do that with my family. I feel stuck.

In 1959, my dad starts the House of Note violin shop. He puts a telephone on my uncle's desk and starts making phone calls. We don't have the money we used to but Mom and Dad are happier. They talk about everyday things instead of yelling, and Mom tells Dad how proud she is of him. Dad has been invited to play in the Pablo Casals Festival of Music in Puerto Rico. He is the only person from the Midwest to be invited. He has to borrow money from my Aunt Lottie to go. Lottie never lets him forget it. She calls and says, "How can you go to Puerto Rico when you never help with expenses for your mother in the nursing home?" She doesn't understand that he is getting his soul back. I can tell that he feels important again by the way he tells everyone he knows that he is going. He is back in touch with his friends from New York and the music world and getting some self-esteem back. I wish something like that could happen to me.

He and Mom go for six weeks every spring. I stay with Naomi. I don't like it. He tells me how much fun it is for him to go to Puerto Rico and says, "I just love to gamble." He plays craps after the concerts. He shows me the coffee can he saves quarters in. This is the money he takes for gambling. After a few years he tells me "I won so much the armed guard had to walk me to the safety deposit box." And the next year he says, "I'm paying off what I lost all year long." The quarters aren't quite enough. Mom loves going to Puerto Rico. She starts planning and packing, putting a clothes-stand in the extra bedroom to hang her clothes on. She packs everything with tissue paper so it doesn't wrinkle.

When I'm seventeen, I get my first part time job. Selling clothes in a little women's shop in downtown Minneapolis called "Three Sisters." I take the still dreaded bus downtown, but get to drive home with Dad. We listen to "Point of Law." Point of Law is a three-minute daily program featuring compelling courtroom cases and fascinating legal decisions that affect all our lives. We don't talk about the show just listen every day. I like this time with him; I feel more connected.

I'm not very good at selling because I don't want to approach anyone to see if they need help. I just stand around waiting for someone to ask me for help. My grandfather had started an allowance for me when I was little. Twenty-five cents a week. Now its up to $5.00 a week. After I start working, I tell my grandfather "I don't need my allowance anymore now that I am working." He says, "I'm very, very proud of you." A couple years later, I tell him "I'm going to go to New York with some friends." He says, " You know you have money." "What do you mean?" I ask. He says, "I have been putting your allowance in the bank for you every week." I did not know that he had done that. I use it to go on my trip.

Judy and I haven't seen too much of each other since eighth grade because of what happened, And she has a boyfriend which takes up a lot of her time. Then she breaks her hip horseback riding and calls and says, "Will you take the cab with me to school and carry my books?" She can't climb up the stairs on the bus. I walk over every morning. I have missed her. We talk like we were never apart. We talk about school, new friends, her boyfriend--whatever comes to mind. I feel accepted and am glad I can help her. Even happier that she called me. We ride the cab together for a few months until she can get up the stairs of the school bus.

Mom says, " If you ever start smoking, please tell me. Don't keep it a secret." My sister had started smoking when she was young, and they were always catching her smoking in her bedroom and putting butts out her windows into the gutters. I am down in a friend's basement and she is teaching me how to smoke. How to hold it, how to inhale. We think we look pretty cool with those little Kent regulars. I go home and tell Mom, "I started smoking today." I see her disappointment, but she all she says is OK. I don't smoke in front of her for years. I learned to smoke well. It takes me thirty years to quit.

I start my senior year in high school and I have a group of friends that I like, even though inside I don't feel like I belong. They ask me to do things all the time. Deep down, I think it's because I can get the car whenever I want. For the first time, Dad has let me take our car, a tan chrysler station wagon, to school, we decide to skip school. We drive over to another high school in the city to see some kids we know. As we walk in, there is no one is in the halls except a finger-pointing teacher hysterically yelling, "Where do you belong?" She drags us into the principal's office and lines us up in a row. "What are your names and what school did you come from?" the principal asks. Everyone gives a fake name. One of the gals gives the name of a Mouseketeer from the TV show, The Micky Mouse Club. The principal asks, "Who's driving?" I have to show my driver's license. I am the only one who gets caught. The school has been calling my mother telling her I am not in school. She is hysterical calling back crying "Have you found my daughter yet?" It terrifies her not knowing where I am. I have always been the good little girl. Needless to say I never drive to school again. They take the car away and ground me for a short time. Mom looks so sad. I can tell how disappointed she is in me. I have never done anything like this before. I followed the rules and did what I was supposed to, until now.

I am walking down the hall to skip school again. I haven't learned much from the first time. We don't have a car, but we are on our way over to McDonalds to have a cigarette in the bathroom. I feel something hit my mouth. I put my tongue up and feel a hole. My front tooth is half gone. There is no pain and I can't quite figure out what has happened. The teeth on either side are perfect, not a scratch. My friend says, "One of the boys from the shop class must have thrown something. It hit you in the mouth." The only thing on the floor is a penny. It cut my front tooth in half. I go to the nurse and they call Mom. Off to the dentist we go. It is going to be a long process to get my tooth fixed, so I have a temporary cap on it. I use the accident to my advantage. As I walk into history class, I pull off the temporary cap. I go up to the teacher and point at my tooth and say, "I have to go to the dentist." "For sure, get going. I'll write you a pass," the teacher says. I head into the bathroom, lock myself into a stall, stand on the stool and have a cigarette. Afterwards, I put the temporary cap back on and just walk into my next class as if nothing had happened. I graduated by the skin of my teeth, literally.

It's August, 1962, the summer after graduation and the same girls and I are on our way to Somerset, Wisconsin, in Dad's car. He finally let me use it again. We want to drink, and the drinking age in Wisconsin is eighteen. We drink 3.2 beer and get happy and silly. I lie to my dad about where we are going. On the way home, with everyone asleep in the back seat, I see flashing red lights behind me. My heart starts pounding. The policeman is standing at the window writing me a speeding ticket. He asks, "Have you heard that Marilyn Monroe died?" I think who cares about that? My father is going to kill me. A few weeks later I get a notice that I have to go to court in Wisconsin. Dad gets the letter first. He is pretty disappointed, but I don't get punished. All he says is, "Having to go to court and paying the fine is punishment enough." I can tell he is disappointed in me. He looks so sad. I think, "When will I stop disappointing people?" But, again, I don't know how.

I'm asking Mom if I can use her car. She has a book club meeting at noon but I say, "Can't you get a ride?" I argue with her until she gives in. She always gives in. I drive her to the meeting and she gets a ride home from a friend. Other times I tell her I am sleeping at Kathy's and Kathy tells her mom she is at my house. We go get some of the other girls and drive around Minneapolis and St. Louis Park all night long. Everyone pitches in for gas. It is 25 cents a gallon. Even though we never get caught, I worry all the time about being a disappointment to my parents. They trust me, and I am lying to them all the time.

In 1973-74 I'm still going to Al-Anon and I'm starting to understand how these childhood stories have affected who I am. By sharing them in the meetings and after at coffee, I begin to understand so much more. With everything that has happened, not only to me but to my parents and grandparents, I realize I haven't known how to make good choices.

PART II - LIFE WITH ED

Ed

It is 1963 and I am 19 years old. My girlfriends and I are on our way to their favorite pizza place, I have not been with them before, but they tell me some of the guys we know from DeLaSalle High School usually come. When we get there, I see it is a typical-looking pizza place. Lots of small tables with red and white checked table cloths and plastic glasses for pop. The guys walk in; they are drunk. They come to the table, sit down and start eating pizza. We let them. There is one guy I don't know. He's pretty cute and sits next to me. We talk for a little when he says, " Want to go out?" He seems nice even though he is drunk, so I say yes.

When Ed comes to get me the next night, I can't remember what he looks like and he can't remember my name. When we are in the car, he says, "I went to the wrong house and peaked in a window. There was a woman in the bathtub." He laughed and said he hightailed it out of there to my house a couple doors away.

Ed tells me his family is very strict Catholic and he has five brothers and not much money. We are driving to a movie and Ed says something about a "nigger." I say, "If you ever use that word around me again, we are done." He never does. I surprised myself; I spoke up. I hadn't done that in years.

We spend the next year going to parties at the house of several friends who live away from home. Ed and I still live with our parents. We drink all the time. I love Vodka Tonics and sweet ice cream type drinks like Pink Squirrels. Ed drinks beer and Manhattans. I'm not sure what's in them, but they are strong. He gets drunk a lot, like most of our friends. We have friends, and for the first time in a very long time, I feel like I belong.

Ed is a pretty cool dresser. He wears Gant shirts, khaki pants, and wing tip shoes. He is about six feet tall. His hair is cut close to his head and very short. He has a stocky build, but he's not fat at all. He has hazel eyes and brown hair. His hands are large but very gentle and soft. I love to kiss him, his lips are soft. I am having a blast. We are having a good time, besides having a little sex. We are coming out of the Terrace Theater and are walking back to the car. It is snowing lightly. Ed has on his camel hair long coat. I look up at his profile and say to myself, "I'm going to marry this guy." I have fallen completely and totally in love with him.

It is 2:00 am and a police officer is knocking on the window of Ed's car. We have fallen asleep in front of my house. When we wake up he says, "I thought you were dead." We start parking in out of sight places and have sex in the car. We are parked by the Japanese Gardens at Lake Harriet. Just as we are putting our clothes back on, a very bright light is shining through the window. It is a police officer. He tells us to get lost. I am so scared I almost throw up.

Ed isn't working. He has tried college but didn't like it. He is feeling pretty bad about himself. We talk a little about what he wants to do with his life, but he doesn't know. He has had a couple of jobs, but he doesn't like those either. He's not working right now. I'm not doing too well in the self-esteem department either. I am still mad at my mom from when I was sixteen, but I think I'm really mad at myself. I have gained some weight and really don't like who I am and wondering why Ed likes me. I began to think it is the sex. His parents tell him, "You either get a job, or go into the army." He decides on the army. He's getting ready to leave for basic training, and I am feeling very sad. Will this end our relationship? Will I ever see him again?

He is at Ft. Leonard Wood for basic training, and I am on a Greyhound bus on my way to see him for a long weekend. I am hot and sticky and it's not very romantic. I check into a pretty seedy motel, the only one that is close to the base. He calls but can't get over to see me as much as we want. I sit in the motel by myself and watch TV. It's so hot I don't want to be outside. Ed has only been over to see me twice. He didn't realize he couldn't take the weekend off. We had sex and then he went back to base. I'm on the bus home and I am pretty disappointed. It was not a good weekend.

Ed is home for a month on leave, and we take up right where we left off going to parties and having fun. This is what seems to be the most important: having fun. He tells me he is being sent to Germany for two years.

Ed and I are in the car. He says, "I was engaged once, but it didn't work out." I say, "Can I see the ring?" He doesn't answer. A few nights later he says, "Here I brought the ring. Why don't you keep it?" I did. I am now engaged. I'm not happy about the way we got engaged. He never really asked me to marry him. But this is all I have ever wanted--to get married and have a family of my own. It is a couple of nights later when he tells me his mother. Lila was waiting up for him, and when he walked into the house, she said, " Do you always zip up your pants on the way into the house? Who is she?" He really doesn't answer her. He doesn't know what to say, but I'm the same way. I have no voice. He doesn't tell her we are engaged. I am happy to be engaged but feel guilty, like I forced Ed to bring me the ring. It's not quite like losing a glass slipper on a ballroom step.

Ed has left for Germany and I am so lonely I can hardly stand it. I am writing to him every day. I also get letters every day. He is as lonely as I am and says, "Why don't you come to Germany and we will get married." All I ever wanted was to get married. I didn't like school, so college was out for me. In the 1960's all any of us girls wanted was to get married and have kids like most of our mom's. I think I wanted to feel loved and accepted. If someone—anyone-- wanted to marry me, then I must be OK. Cinderella is a big part of that. Is Ed my prince? Of course I say, "Yes!"

Ed and I have been together for a year. I have never met his parents. In one of his letters he says I should call them and ask if I can come over. They have no idea who I am.

I walk into Ed's parent's house and introduce myself. I am scared to death. My hands are shaking. My heart is pounding. I have no idea how they will react to me. Not only am I going to tell them that Ed and I are going to get married, but that I am Jewish. They look very skeptical. Who is this girl they know is having sex with their son but have never met? I sit down on the edge of the big old mission chair in their living room. It has wide wood arms that feel way too big for me. Lila is walking in from the kitchen with a very large piece of very white meringue covered with canned cherries. I hate cherries but I eat the whole thing. I begin, "Ed and I are engaged. He wants me to come to Germany, and I have said I will." They are visibly upset. Now I say, "I am Jewish." I have not really thought about what it takes to talk with them. I just do it. Somehow my voice comes back a little shaky, but I speak. Ed has stressed how important religion is to his parents. Lila and Ed (Ed's dad) tell me, "You will have to go to classes at our church to learn about our religion or you can't get married." Lila makes arrangements for us to go to these classes. and we start going together once a week for six weeks. She says, "I don't expect you to go alone." I have to sign papers saying I will raise my children Catholic. At first it is no big deal. I have no religion per se, but Ed's is strong. As Lila and I get to know each other and attend these classes it dawns on me for the first time how important being Jewish is to me. It is my heritage; it is who I am. I remember the holidays. They are so important to me I could never give them up. They are good memories of my childhood, being with family, eating good food and celebrating. I tell Lila, "I hope you understand that I agree to raise my children Catholic, but I can never become Catholic myself." She says, "I understand." I think in this moment, similar to the moment I knew I loved Ed and wanted to marry him, I knew Lila and I would be friends. We really like each other and it has surprised both of us. I am beginning to understand the depth of what being Jewish means to me.

Mom and Dad and I are having dinner together sitting at the dining room table. I tell them "Ed want's me to come to Germany and get married there." I am very excited but my parents look scared. They aren't very happy either. I can tell by the look on Mom's face that she is worried about me. But my mother knows that if she tries to stop me, she will only push me further away. I know this because of a call I hear from my Aunt Lottie. She says to my mother, "How can you allow her to do this?" Mom's answer: "How can I not?"

My parents want to meet Ed's mom and dad. The five of us are sitting in the living room of the big house. Dad is sitting in the armchair with his leg thrown over the arm. He is trying to be so nonchalant. Mom and I are on the edge of the couch. The first thing Ed's dad says is, "Is there any reason you are leaving for Germany so quickly?" inferring that I am pregnant. Dad's face turns red. He takes his leg off the arm of the chair and sits straight up. I can hear my mother's intake of breath. Ed's parents don't know that my sister had run away and gotten married because she was pregnant. My parents have tried to keep a tight rein on me so the same thing doesn't happen. Dad responds, "If she were pregnant, she would leave tomorrow not three months from now." What he doesn't know is that it is only by the grace of GOD that I am not.

Mom and Dad try to make this experience as normal as they can, if that is possible. We stage a picture taking session with the family and friends that would be in my wedding if it were in Minneapolis, not Germany. Including Ed's family. Ed is in Germany, so he is not a part of the celebration.

I am standing in my wedding dress with my sister and two of my friends from high school. They are wearing borrowed royal blue taffeta bridesmaid dresses and little rimmed hats with lace that comes over their foreheads. Ed's parents are also here, along with Ed's younger brothers. Kevin, the youngest, is not yet a year old. My grandparents are also included. Mom has hired a photographer to take pictures of this incomplete wedding party.

It's early December and Mom and Dad are throwing a party for all their friends and the rest of the family to celebrate my getting married. As hard as they try, I know how devastated they are to have another daughter getting married and they can't be there. We don't talk about it, but I can tell by the looks on their faces that they are trying to be happy. But it doesn't quite come across as real.

Germany

Wedding Day

It's a cold January day in 1964. My parents drive me to the airport and watch as I get on an airplane bound for Frankfurt, Germany, my wedding dress in hand to meet Ed. In Germany I get off the plane. No Ed. I feel that all too familiar tightening in my stomach. Fear. All this is so contradictary. Such fear, but I take a plane to get married and to Germany no less. I pace the airport for what seems like an hour until I see Ed running across the airport with a stranger he introduces as Sergeant Bills. We drive back to the little town of Segelsbach, where Ed is stationed.

A friend of Ed's has a little one-room cottage with a coal stove and not much light that we can use until we get married. The living room has a wood table and four chairs. I am so scared I don't even look at the rest of the place. Ed can't stay. He says, "I have to go back to base. They won't let me stay over. I can only come after I'm done with my duty at around five pm." I am left all alone. We are supposed to get married on Sunday after I get there, only the paper work has been held up. German law says that we have to be married by the German consulate in addition to our church wedding.

The night I arrive it is dark and snowy, so I don't get to see the little town. But the next day I can see there is a main street with little shops and wonderful little houses in the distance. It is all covered in snow, just like home. I wish I had the nerve to pull on my boots and go out to explore, but I'm too afraid. What if they find out I'm Jewish? Will they throw things at me? Will they scream at me? What would people do? Instead I sit at the wooden table and write letter after letter to my mom.

I am as lonely or even more so then I have ever been. Some days I write up to ten letters to my mom, pouring out all the loneliness and sadness I am feeling. I keep wondering if leaving home and coming to Germany was the right decision? I'm not so sure. After a week or so, Sergeant Bills tells Ed, "You can't just leave her out there all alone." He tells him to bring me to their apartment, which is on base in Heilbronn, a small town about twenty minutes away. They want me to stay with them until our church wedding. It feels so much safer, and I'm not all alone. They are wonderful and welcoming. Ed comes to visit and after the family goes to sleep. We make love on their couch. I am so afraid to say no, even though I don't feel right about it. Will Ed hate me or leave me if I say no? I don't know the answer to that question, so I don't say anything. It is February 1,

1964, one month after I got to Germany, and I am getting ready for our church wedding.

We got married by the German Consulate a few days ago. The ceremony took about ten minutes. Afterward, we went to dinner with Ed's friends and Sergeant Bills and his wife. Ed got drunk.

Mrs. Bills helps me get dressed before we go to church. It is so windy that as I get out of the car my veil almost blows off. Their fourteen-year-old daughter is standing up for me. Ed's friend is his best man. I don't know anyone else, and as I think about walking down the aisle in front of everyone I almost throw up. I almost throw up a lot whenever I think of what I am doing, but it doesn't stop me.. As I peek into the church through a little window at the top of the door, I count twelve people. Stiff upper lip and onward down the aisle I go thinking, "What's the big deal?"

We have a photographer at the wedding, and I send copies to my whole family, even to my grandparents, Dad's parents in Chicago. I include pictures of us kneeling at the altar, not understanding how they would feel seeing me being married by a Catholic priest.

Our First Year

Ed is a private so we can't get housing on base. We rent the third floor apartment of a house in Heilbronn.

We are walking home from our first grocery shopping trip to the PX, the grocery store on base, carrying four large bags of groceries. Ed drops one of the bags. "I told you not to buy so much!" he yells as he storms off. I am left to carry one bag home and return to pick up the mess that is left. I really begin to wonder what I have gotten myself into. Is he really this mean? I haven't seen it before.

Our landlady, Frau Esch, is a wonderful woman. We are talking one day, and I say, "I'm Jewish." She says, "I didn't know anything about the war and how the Jews were treated. None of us did. The war was so far away we didn't know about the Jews." I can tell by her voice that she is ashamed even though she doesn't say it out loud. If she isn't, then why would she have to explain?

There are three floors in her home with shiny wood slippery stairs all the way up. We have to polish

Frau Esh

them every week. She also has us put the rugs out on the railing and beat them once a month. The living room is the only room that has heat, from a small coal stove. Frau Esch tells us to wrap the coal in wet paper at night to keep it going until morning. As I go down to the basement to carry up a bucket of coal, I am reminded of how much I hate basements. These are all things she wants us to do to help keep the house clean while we rent from her.

Our bedroom is big with a huge bed and a wonderful down cover called a featherbed to keep us warm. There is a wonderful old dresser with a mirror and no heat. The bathroom has no running water except for the toilet. Ed is getting ready for work, and I am filling two basins with hot water that I warmed up on the stove so he can shave. The kitchen is a tiny space, cupboards on one side with a small shallow sink underneath and a small stove on the other side. I have to heat water in a big silver metal wash-tub to wash dishes. I have brought a few pictures and a very few knick-knacks with me to try make this our home. I must be doing a good job, because our home becomes the hang out for all Ed's friends from the base. Following in my grandparent's tradition, they come for dinner many Sunday afternoons. We are such a long way from home that we all become fast friends. Even Frau Esch comes for dinner.

Coal Stove

Gregory Michael

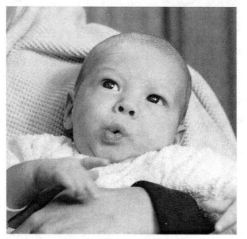

Greg's Passport Picture

Maybe I got pregnant that night on the couch at Sargent Bills. I'm not sure but I never get my period. When I write mom and tell her I am pregnant, she writes back, "I'm very sad that I can't come to Germany when the baby is born, but I'm not well enough." She says her diabetes has gotten worse and she can't travel.

I am eight months pregnant and we are on a bus traveling with our new friends, Helen and Bob, to Austria, Switzerland, and Liechtenstein. Our first night is in the Swiss Alps, and as night falls someone is standing on the mountain blowing an elk horn. There are little window boxes on the houses in town that remind me of the book

Heidi. What an adventure we are having. I'm hoping things will be better for us. The travel bug had bitten me. I want it to never stop. I want to see the whole world. China, Australia, Greece an African safari. I want to have more adventures like this one .

When we get home, I still have morning sickness though I'm over eight months pregnant, and I can't get out of bed without having a cracker first. I am at the stove in the kitchen fixing fried chicken for the boys from base. I am running to the bathroom to throw up every few minutes. Mike comes in and says, "Here let me cook that. You don't look so good." It just occurs to me that Ed never comes to help. But I don't ask for help either.

Ed and I are lying in bed. He says, "What if there is something wrong with the baby?" "Oh, I'm sure everything will be fine," I say. Why is Ed so very worried there will be something wrong? I have no idea and we don't talk about it.

We just got home from a movie on base. I've changed my clothes and am getting into bed and my water breaks. Ed is so nervous he breaks the zipper on his pants trying to get them on. Three pairs later we are waking up our neighbors downstairs who have agreed to drive us to Stuttgart where the army hospital is. It's about one and a half hours away. I am lying down in the back seat. Ed is sitting by the window with my legs over his lap. No one is talking. It's very quiet in the car. I am just trying to hold in the yelling from the pain. It started so quickly, right after my water broke. By the time we arrive, I am in hard labor. I can hardly get out of the car it hurts so much. Ed gets help, and they wheel me up to labor and delivery in a wheel chair. The pain is so bad I am bent over in the chair. After they settle us into a room, I am yelling at Ed, "This is all your fault, never again." Greg is born five hours later. It's October 7th, 1964.

When I see him for the first time, he has this incredible pointed head. Scared to death, I ask the doctor, "What is wrong with him?"

He says "Oh! Don't worry, we will shape his head. It is just from the birth. He is fine." Well, Ed walks in and when he sees Greg he turns a strange color of grey. I, very calmly like I am the expert, but shaking inside, tell him, "The doctor says he is just fine." Neither of us believes it. They have just brought Greg in to me after cleaning him up, and his head is perfect. There is certainly nothing wrong with him. We are in the army hospital. Ed has gone home because he has to report to work at the base. He will come back when its time for us to come home. Greg is in a little bassinet right next to me. He is screaming. I am so tired I can hardly move. It's 2:00 AM and he has been crying for a day and a half. A nurse walks in and says, "Would you like me to take him for a little while so you can sleep?" PLEASE. After two straight days of crying, we are home.

Home with Greg

Home at last Greg is in a little crib in the main room with the coal heater and it is nice and warm. I am putting a mirror up to his mouth to make sure he is still breathing. He has slept so much since we got home, I have to wake him to eat. He is an angel. Today I am washing diapers in the wash-tub on the stove. I'm using a plunger to make sure they are clean. Life is not what I expected. But here I am.

We are at another party at some friends' house. Greg is asleep on the bed in the other room. It's Friday night and all our friends are here. Ed drinks a lot. I join in so I feel like I belong.

Several women I have met are sitting and having coffee at our neighbors downstairs at Frau Esch's house. We have become great friends. I think we connect on a level that not many do because we have no one else. I have learned a few German words, but I'm pretty shy about using them. I don't want to look foolish. We are heading downtown to look around and shop a little. We don't have any money. Ed makes $300 a month as a private. I shop. Ed is drinking a lot, and I don't know what to do. It's like he doesn't like me when he drinks. I feel like his mother who does everything for her boys. So I cover up what I am feeling then stuff it down as far as it can go so I don't have to think about the life I am living.

I am trying to deal with this new responsibility, being a mother. Ed is drinking a lot, and he has gained tons of weight. My coming to Germany hasn't helped.

Here we are starting the family I have always dreamt of , but where is Cinderella's prince, my prince? While Ed works at the base, I do everything else--take care of the house, have all his friends over from the base so they can have a good meal, do all the cooking, and take care of Greg. I like doing all of this. It's what my mother did at home and I learned it well. So why am I so angry at Ed. It's Sunday afternoon and the guys are here for dinner. "Leslie," they say, "This food is great. You are terrific." I don't believe them and kind of shrug and say, "Thanks." I have learned well not to speak up or believe nice things.

Letters from Home

I have been in Germany almost a year now, and for the last four to six weeks have had no letters from home. I am worried sick. Is everyone mad at me? Did I do something wrong? I pick up the phone and call Naomi. She answers and is surprised. "What's going on? Why hasn't anyone written for so long?" I ask. Quietly, she says, "Mother has been raped." My mind is racing. How could this happen? I feel guilty immediately because I have written all those sad lonely letters to Mom. I don't dare call Mom. I don't know what I would say. Naomi says, "It's been pretty awful. A man broke into the house while Dad was away working. She was just getting out of the shower and he grabbed her as she was walking into her bedroom. He walked right in the front door. It had been left open a crack when a delivery from the drug store was left. He had a nylon over his head and face."

We have never locked doors or windows in the big house. Mom and Dad always say, "If someone wants to get in all they have to do is break one of the six foot windows in the living room." That night everything changed. Naomi says, "Dad has locked the house up tight." It seems there is so much fear already in our house. How will they deal with this?

Decades later, I saw Anne, a friend of my mother's, at the beauty shop. Out of the blue, she starts talking about the rape. I never heard the story of what happened from anyone. Mom wouldn't talk about it. Other then what Naomi had told me, I didn't know how Mom felt. By the time I got home from Germany, they were trying to forget. Anne said my mom called crying right after it happened and asked, "Will you come over until Ted gets home? He's working tonight." Anne said, "I called the police and went right over." Anne told me that a son of a neighbor was the boy that raped my mother. When the police went to his house, his mother lied and said he was home all evening. She told me they didn't catch him until he had raped several other women and that he's in jail now for a very long time.

On top of the emotions I am feeling about Mom, Ed says, "We have to move to a smaller, cheaper place." I am so sad. I don't want to leave our little third floor apartment and Frau Esch, but we move to a one room apartment with a pull out couch as our bedroom. It's Sunday night. We lie in bed listening to Suspense and Johnny Dollar on the radio. I am far from my friends, missing Frau Esch, and struggling daily with life as it is. Ed is drinking most nights after work, and I am alone, trying to figure out how to be a good mom but not sure I know how. I'm not even sure how to be a good wife. Am I doing something wrong is that why we are not happy, or is the Cinderella story just a dream. No glass slipper for me. I have a baby six months old and I feel so stressed out I call Mom, "Can I come home please? Ed is drinking every night and I am so unhappy. Will you send me money? We don't have any?" She says yes.

I start to think about going home. I am so excited, but I don't feel good about the way I look. I weighed one hundred and seventy-five pounds when Greg was born. I am five foot two inches tall and feel fat and ugly and unloved. It's six months later and I'm still fat. I have started taking diet pills and I haven't slept or eaten much for a month. I've lost the weight, but am wired, anxious and jittery.

When Greg was born, Mom sent us money for a wonderful German pram (buggy). There are a lot of things that I can't take with me, and the buggy is one. I say to Ed, "Whatever you do, don't sell that buggy, bring it home." Ed doesn't say much about my going home. He knows we are not getting along very well, and we never talk about anything important.

Coming Home

I am going home today. I have twenty-five dollars in my pocket for the whole trip. I'm going to stop in Philadelphia to see some friends from Germany whose tour is over and have gone home. Ed only makes $300.00 a month. Twenty-five dollars is all he has for me to take with me on the trip. He is treasurer of the bowling league, and we use that money every month to live on. When he gets home from Germany, he tells me that he had to take out a loan to pay back the league.

The airline I am supposed to fly has gone on strike. They find me a flight on a different airline, but Greg has to sit in my lap. I'm asking the flight attendants to warm up a bottle, but they are so busy with the full plane they don't pay any attention to me. After several tries, I stand up, stick the bottle in a flight attendant's face and yell, "Warm this up!" She does. There is a very nice gentleman sitting a few rows ahead of me. He turns around and says, "Would you like me to hold him for a few hours so you can eat and rest?" Greg is an angel, even with this stranger who is holding him. He sleeps and eats all the way home.

I arrive in New York's JFK airport. I have no idea what to do. I have all my luggage and Greg. I see one of those carts that I can load all the luggage on, and I put Greg on the handle bar. I am pushing it across the airport trying to balance everything. I find the right shuttle to the train station. I'm at Penn Station, and I don't have any idea what to do with all my stuff while I go to buy a train ticket. I decide to leave it in a corner, kind of hidden. Greg and I go to buy a bus ticket. I am walking back to my suitcases and a little old man is standing there and says "You just can't leave things alone here." I almost start to cry. I am so tired and so alone and this nice man has helped me. All I say is thank you. This is such a kindness, much like the man in the airplane who held Greg. I am not used to it.

I'm in a cab on the way to the train station in Philadelphia. I need another cab to take me to Helen and Bob's house. I ask at the customer service desk where to find one. She tells me they are across the bus station and the cab drivers can't come in. "Why not? I will pay them." She says, "Blacks aren't allowed." I again leave my bags alone and walk to the other side of the station, hand Greg to a cab driver and say, "Hold him. I need to get my luggage." I make two trips. I think he is as shocked as I should be, but I'm not afraid that this black man would hurt my son. Forrest Wiggins had been a black man. We load everything in the cab and nothing more is said. I'm at our friends' front door and say, "Got money for a cab?" I spend three wonderful days with them. We had become such good friends in Germany, so it feels like being with family I have not seen for a long time.

I'm on the plane heading home from Philadelphia to Minneapolis. We have seats in the front row. They have attached a little bed to the wall for Greg. We are in the air and he is sound asleep. Somehow everyone on the plane has found out I am coming home from Germany. I wake Greg up I put him in a dark forest green German sweater and pants to match. Everyone on the plane wants me to get off first so they can see the reaction of my family. I am walking off the plane and I see Mom, Dad and Grandma. Even Naomi is smiling. Ed's dad has taken Greg right out of my arms. I start to cry as I get close to Mom. We are crying and hugging. I am so excited to be home.

Mom had asked in a letter what I wanted to eat when I got home. A full delicatessen spread PLEASE... bagel, corn-beef, cream cheese. Grandma Supak's cream and cheese. We are back at the big house and I am home. The table is set with all my favorite foods. Grandma's cream and cheese is a mixture of sour cream and farmer's cheese. It is wonderful. I eat everything. I haven't eaten a full meal for over a month. I have lost twenty five pounds but I'm starving. I have on a green outfit I brought with me to Germany but had not been able to get into. Now it is loose. But I know the diet pills are getting to me and I feel terrible.

I am home staying with my parents without a husband and with a small son. I get a small check from the army because I am an army wife. That is what I live on. I'm not even sure if I remember why I am still mad at Mom. I think I am just mad at life, and I'm not treating her very well. It's like I have become that sixteen-year-old--angry, fearful and mean. Have I ever stopped being sixteen? I don't think so. Mom and I are sitting at the kitchen table eating lunch. I had not planned to ask her but finally say, "How are you after the rape?" She says, "I knew I didn't want to die so I let him do what he wanted so he would leave." I just tell her I am glad she is OK. We never talk about it again. I am so wrapped up in my own life, I don't even think about what it has done to hers until years later. I revert back to being a teenager. I want to use the car and do the same thing to her I did when I was in high school. I ask and ask until she gives in. She even calls a friend to come get her for her book club. She never says anything, and always gives in.

I have to go to Naomi's for three weeks. My parents are taking their yearly trip to Puerto Rico. I don't want to go to Naomi's, but they don't want me to stay in the house alone. Naomi has asked me to take care of her kids, who are eight, six, four and two years old, several times since I have been here. Greg is a little over six months, so its a big task. Naomi hasn't said anything, but it feels like she wants me to do this every time she goes out. I think, "Why can't she get a babysitter?" But I don't say anything. I just go along. I have no voice when it comes to taking care of myself. I take a look at my life, and I don't like what I see, but I don't do anything about it. I don't know what to do. I just do what others want, whether I like it or not. How would Naomi know what I am feeling? I don't talk about it, and I'm not even sure I know myself. Naomi wants us to live side by side when Ed gets home, and I do know instinctively that can never happen. I want a life of my own.

Ed Comes Home

I'm on my way to pick up Ed at the airport. We have not talked to each other in six months. We have written letters, but that's all. I don't recognize him because he has gained so much weight. We are going to stay with my parents for a month, and then we are going to Tacoma, Washington for the last six months of Ed's tour. It never occurs to me not to go. I ask Ed about the buggy. He says, "I sold it to go to Munich with the boys." I am furious. I scream at him "How could you do that? It was the only thing I asked you to bring home, and you didn't do it." He doesn't respond.

We have been in Tacoma for a few weeks in an apartment off base. I thought it was bad in Germany! At least I had friends in Germany. It is October and we will be here until May, the rainy season. We only have one car, so I can't go anywhere. We have had only two days of sun. Ed is drinking every night with his buddies from the base and not coming home until late most nights. I call Mom and say, "Please can I come home?" She says, "No, you have to deal with your life as it is." REALLY? How am I to do that? Nothing has changed for me. Cinderella is now out of my range of thinking. No one tells you what happens after she marries the prince.

Ed walks in the door one evening and asks what the box is by the wall. I say, "A vacuum cleaner salesmen came by today and I bought one." He is furious. "You spent three hundred dollars on a vacuum cleaner when we have no money." "I enjoyed talking to the salesmen so much I bought the vacuum. That's how lonely I am," he doesn't respond. I am beginning to think he doesn't know what to say when I get upset. We start to pawn it every third week of the month to get the money to live on and get it back on payday. We had that vacuum for years. It was the best vacuum I have ever had.

We are getting ready to go home. I can't wait. This has been the longest six months of my life. We put the crib mattress in the back seat so Greg could play and sleep and stop at the pawn shop to see if the vacuum is still there, it is we put it in the trunk and head for home.

Ed is driving crazy, he just wants to get home and hardly stops except for bathroom breaks. It's pitch black and we are on a windy mountain road in the middle of the night and we get a flat tire. We are unpacking the trunk to find the jack and it doesn't work. A car comes by, the only one we have seen and stops. He drives us to a little motel not far away tucked into the side of the mountain. The people are so nice and even get a crib for Greg. I'm not used to these small kindness. Not many people have been kind to me in my life only a few like mom, dad, grandma and grandpa. I think I am a kind person and want to be treated the same way I treat others. It just doesn't seem to happen even in my marriage. It's morning and as I look out the window I see this amazing, beautiful view of the mountain. They help us get the tire fixed and we are on the road again. We decide to drive straight through. We just want to get home. We are going to stay with Mom and Dad again until Ed finds a job. I'm thinking the Army is done now and life will get better.

Ed has gotten a job in the shipping department at Rogness Equipment Co. We are in a one bedroom apartment in Minneapolis, across the street from the main beach at Cedar Lake where I had spent so much time when I was younger. He is still drinking and we fight all the time. We fight about money., about what I spend whether it is on food or clothes or something for Greg. Although he never drinks during the week, on weekends he starts drinking on Friday night and continues to drink all weekend. We also fight about this. because I don't want to be left home alone on the weekends. He feels remorseful on Sunday and goes to work on Monday.

Elizabeth Ann

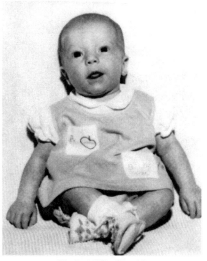

Beth 2 Weeks old

Greg is such a happy kid. I put him in his crib for a nap after lunch and he wakes up maybe two hours later and just plays. Around 4:30 or 5:00, he calls out "Mommy up." Maybe I am doing something right but I think it is just the kind of child he is. He is the only joy I feel. It doesn't feel like I have much joy in my life. Maybe with everything that is going on I don't know what joy is. I only know I love this little boy with all my heart and will do anything to protect him from anything and anyone. We are going to move to St. Louis Park into a two bedroom apartment because I am pregnant again.

I'm not feeling as sick as I did with Greg although I have been spotting a little. It's about a week before my due date. I am so sick of being pregnant. At my doctor appointment I tell her that and she says, "I will strip your membranes and if the baby is ready to come you will go into labor tonight," I did. We have moved and I'm stressed. It's about midnight and I say to Ed, "I think we have to go to the hospital. I'm in labor." He says, "We can't go yet. We haven't picked out a girl's name." I say, "sorry we have to go now." Elizabeth Ann is born at 3:00 am on February 10, 1967. This little girl is the prettiest thing I have ever seen. No pointed head for her. She's a little hesitant to be here and lets us know. She has been crying for five hours. The next day the doctor says, "I stayed with her because I thought we were going to lose her we couldn't get her to stop crying." I feel guilty because I had her induced. I think she just wasn't ready to be born no matter what the doctor said. I still am not sure what joy is but I look at this little girl and my heart gets bigger. Now I have two children to protect and love, but I'm not sure I know how.

She is the first girl in fifty eight years on the Volker side so everyone is very excited. Her Grandma Lila finally has a little girl she can make dresses for and just cuddle. Grandma Lila would have named a daughter Elizabeth but only had boys. Six of them. So we named her Elizabeth, calling her Beth right from the start. She has the most beautiful red hair and the cutest little face you have ever seen. She is like a little angel, but does she ever cry.....She cries for the first nine months. She will not go to anyone but me.

When she is two weeks old I say to Ed, "I want to get out a little bit, Greg is all ready for bed and Beth is fed and changed and sleeping." I head over to Southdale shopping center just to walk around. I walk in two hours later and she is screaming. Ed says, "She started to cry the minute you left and cried the whole time you were gone.

You can never leave her with me again." I laugh a little take her from him and say in a little voice, "You little stinker, you go to sleep." As I lay her down in her crib, she falls asleep. Ed can't believe what he is seeing.

How will I do this? The mother of two kids and I still don't have a clue about myself. How am I going to raise these kids when I have all this fear that I never deal with? And no voice to talk about it. I'm still not sure where the fear comes from but I feel frightened all the time. Will I be a good mother? Does Ed still love me? Can I make a good home for us? So many unanswered questions.

I'm on my way to pick Ed up from work. I pull into a 7-Eleven to get cigarettes and leave the car running with Greg and Beth in the car. I look out to check on them and the car is rolling and I run to stop it. If it had not hit the fire-hydrant on the corner my kids would have been in the middle of a very busy street at 5:00 pm. What kind of mother am I? I wasn't sure.

Sarcoid

Greg is five years old and Beth is two and a half. I'm sick. I haven't felt good for about a month. I have been to the doctor but they can't find anything wrong. I have no energy and am listless. I haven't done anything all day I don't even have the energy to wash out the dirty diapers so I leave them in the toilet. Ed just came home from work, "You don't look so good," he says. Ed calls the doctor and they tell him to bring me right to the hospital.

I have been in the hospital for a week. Lila has the kids because Ed has to work. I have lots of tests I don't even know what most of them are for. They come in and say, "We want to do a liver biopsy. We think you have tuberculosis." about an hour later they come at me with the longest needle I have ever seen. They put some kind of anesthetic on the spot and the needle goes in. It doesn't hurt but I can feel the pressure when they pull it out. After they get the results they come in again and say, "You will have to be here at least two more weeks, you have Sarcoid." What the heck is that? I have never heard of it. They tell Ed and me that it is a virus. It can hit different people in different ways and it has hit my lungs. I'm still smoking and the doctors tell me I have to quit. Ed comes every night and says "You are not supposed to be smoking," and takes my pack of cigarettes and throws them away. After he leaves, I go downstairs to the vending machine and buy another pack. I can still buy them in the hospital. I just can't quit. I think about why I can't quit and for the first time I realize they are a crutch for all the pent up feeling that I have. The doctors put me on prednisone. We are moving into our very own house the next week and I have to be here. I start to cry and cry for two days. All the sadness I feel about my life is right in my chest. Not only am I crying about having to stay but where has my Cinderella story gone?

My grandfather has given us a down payment to buy a house. All the grandchildren have a choice: money for college, a wedding or a down payment. He gave us fifteen hundred dollars. Our house cost twenty thousand dollars and we have no idea how we can afford it.

Our Little House

Ed's mom and my mom pack everything from the apartment and clean the new house and put everything away. Ed has just dropped me off after getting out of the hospital with the kids. I have to be on prednisone for at least a year. They have told me this is the only cure. If I stay on this medication for at least a year, this should go away. I have not quit smoking.

I call Ed an hour later and say, "Where in the hell are their toys?" I couldn't find anything! I sit down and cry some more. I love this house, our little three bedroom expansion. It is two houses behind the bowling alley. We can hear the pins drop when the back door is open. It's all ours but it's starting out wrong. My marriage is falling apart not only because I am sick but Ed is drinking a lot. We don't know what the problem is. What could it be? Is it all of the above? New house, drinking, my health and two kids. We are so unsettled and unhappy and now I feel even worse about myself because it's a month later and I have gained twenty five pounds and have full acne from the medication I'm on..

Greg is five years old when we move into the house. We find out many years later that on the first day we moved in, he went down the block to every house and knocked on the door and said, "Hi, my name is Greg. We just moved in. Can I see your house?" That's our boy.

A Car

My grandfather has had a massive heart attack. My grandmother is in the same hospital for something else. He tells my dad that he can't live without her and thinks she is going to die. She survives; he doesn't. My grandmother has given me my grandfather's car. My mother can't drive any longer because she has lost her eye sight due to the diabetes. My grandmother pays for everything as long as I drive my mother and her anywhere they need to go. We go grocery shopping once a week to three different stores and I take my mother to the beauty shop once a week. I don't mind taking them. We have a pretty good time running around and I have a car. Before I got the car, I was driving Ed to work if I need to go somewhere.

Money

Ed and I still have no money and it is a sore spot for us ever since the grocery shopping in Germany. Ed thinks I spend too much and I basically have no money of my own because I don't work. "Ed, can I have a dollar for cigarettes?" He says, "Why do you need a dollar? They are only 25 cents a pack."

Anita

My Wonderful Friend

We have been in the house for a year and I am walking down the block with a cake to introduce myself to the new neighbors that are moving in. I meet Anita that day. We hit it off. We are getting together most morning for coffee after the kids are off to school, Greg is six years old and in first grade. Beth is home with me. I am twenty two years old I tell her how unhappy I am.

"I don't know what is wrong. We just fight all the time. It's like Ed doesn't like me anymore." She just listens. It's just what I need.

Anita is Swedish and she has this wonderful accent. I walk down to see her and she is talking on the phone to her family in Sweden.

I have no idea what she is saying. I just love to hear her talk. She is becoming the sister I always wanted.

Anita and Bob live two houses away from us. They have two boys. Steve and Mike. They are a few years older then our kids. The four of us, Anita, Bob Ed and I get along really well. We start doing thing together. Going to parties or just getting together for dinner at each others homes. Some of Anita's family comes once a year. There are twelve children in her family. She has a twin brother. They love to go shopping so we all go out together. Usually out to lunch and shopping. After a few years when we are both working we meet after we get home and go for a walk together just about everyday. She is the closes friend I have ever had.

The Neighborhood

We are becoming friends with several couples on the block and go to parties together most Friday nights. Everyone drinks and it does not seem to be a problem for them. Yet at our house, it is getting more and more difficult. Ed's behavior when he drinks is so different then when he is sober. He gets mean and nasty and very critical of me when he drinks. I don't see the other couples arguing like we do. Maybe they are I just don't see it.

Ed calls from the police station to tell me he has had a car accident. He's drunk. I call Dad, "Can you come with me to the police station? Ed has been arrested?" We get Ed out of jail after dad pays the fine. We don't say anything. This is not the first time he has helped us. Dad calls the next day and says, "I have a friend that would like to come talk to you." We are sitting in the kitchen and Morrie says, "I think alcohol is the problem." We say, "Absolutely not, Ed only drinks on weekends." We talk about what an alcoholic looks like. Ed says, "It's a person who is falling down drunk and can't hold a job. I have a job and only drink on the weekends never during the week." Morrie leaves and the conversation is over.

We are at a friend's house for a party in Golden Valley and Ed is really drunk. We get in the car and are fighting about his driving. I say, "Let me drive or let me out." He pulls the car over on Highway 100 and Golden Valley Road and says, "Then get out." It is after midnight.

I am walking up the exit ramp with no clue what I am going to do. I have no money and no way to call a cab. A car pulls up beside me. I start shaking. Will I get raped like Mom? He rolls down his window and says, "You look like you are in trouble." "OH! NO! I'm fine," I say as the tears are running down my face. He says, "I will not hurt you. I will drive you home and I swear I will not hurt you." I sit as close to the window of the car in case I have to jump out. He did just what he said he would and as I tell him what has happened. I cry and cry all the way home. Once again like at the train station in New York, a stranger shows me kindness which I almost refuse being still so suspicious of anyone who is nice to me. How can this be happening?

When I get home, I send the babysitter home and Ed is not there yet. I run around the house locking all the doors and windows, forgetting about the window in Greg's room upstairs. Ed gets home a few minutes later and is trying to get in. He puts a ladder up to Greg's window. I run up the stairs to lock it and Greg wakes up. Greg says in his sleepy little voice, "Why won't you let Daddy in." Calmly, I say, "I'm just playing a joke on Daddy. It's OK, you can go back to bed." I go downstairs and let Ed in. I'm feeling terrible. Nothing is said. I just go to bed.

How could I do this to a five year old? I don't recognize how crazy my behavior has gotten. When Ed drinks, he behaves a certain way but what the heck is wrong with me? We still don't see the problem. Although it is not fun anymore, we still go to parties and drink a lot.

Pat lives at the other end of the block. I think we have become pretty good friends and we see each other almost every day. She and her husband start coming to all the parties. Life on Virginia Avenue is getting crazier by the day. Anita and I still spend as much time as we can together and other friends are joining us. We get together for coffee in the morning since none of us work. It feels a little like

Germany. We all become very good friends. We tell each other everything. I complain to Pat and Anita how awful life is. I think Ed doesn't care about me because I have gotten fat. He has gone on a diet and lost all his extra weight. Anita says, "Maybe if you try harder to lose the weight, things will get better." I start to diet again this time without the pills. I start counting calories and lose about twenty five pounds but it doesn't help our relationship much. My body image is still so bad. I count every morsel that goes into my mouth. Driving everyone crazy including myself. When I go for a walk for every mile I walk I take off one hundred calories from my total calories for the day never having more than one thousand calories total for any given day. Never really eating more than twelve hundred. Ed and I never talked about anything; we are just mad at each other all the time. I wish we could talk about our hopes and dreams for the future. What we want for ourselves and what we want for our children. We don't plan anything out we just live by the seat of our pants.

A New Crisis

It's Friday night and we are walking home from a neighborhood party. Ed is really drunk and mumbles, "I really want her." Who is he talking about, what is happening? At first I don't understand, then it clicks. I am so mad and hurt I say, "Go ahead, who cares." He says, "I have." As we walk the block to our house I act like I don't care but I am devastated. My heart feels like it is broken. If I thought things were bad before, this is the worst. He is having an affair with one of the neighbors. I didn't understand when this woman, who I thought was a friend came up the block to our house around 4:00 PM to talk that she was really waiting to see Ed when he got home from work. I guess even a glimpse is enough for her. It all starts to make sense.

What can I do? LEAVE? How can I do that? I have no job, no money, two kids and all this fear. Fear, insecurity, money: it is all hitting me in the face. There is a part of Ed that knows how much I am hurting and can't stand it. The look in his eyes is full of pain, I can see it. We are lying in bed and I ask, "What is she like in bed? Does she do things I don't?" I think if I understand what she is doing that I'm not it will help us. He doesn't want to tell me but I insist as I cry. It doesn't help.

He tells me a few months later the affair is over but it isn't and I find some evidence. I confront him, "Are you still seeing her?" He says, "Yes." Somehow I always know when it has started up again.

Maybe it is his drinking patterns that give it away I'm not sure but I always find out eventually. Why am I still here? I don't think I have any other choice. I don't find out until later that everyone knew but didn't want to say anything. I still complain to Anita and she still just listens.

Ed calls Friday night saying "I'm going out with the boys for a drink." I reply, "Do what you want I don't care." I have lined up our babysitter to come take care of the kids if he calls last minute. I have a friend whose husband works Friday nights and we go out drinking. We start meeting up with Ed in the bars. He doesn't like it.

We are walking into the Leaning Post, a bar in St. Louis Park. They have a dance floor on the right as you walk in and the other dark lit space is filled with tables. There are always a lot of people at the Leaning Post; it is a popular place to be. As my friend and I look around the room for other friends, I see Ed sitting at a table with the woman he is supposedly not having the affair with but again I realize he is seeing her again. I walk right up to the table. "So how is the fucking bitch of the neighborhood?" I ask. What a way to get my voice back. Ed is a shocking shade of white. I turn around and walk out. I find her car, open up the hood and start pulling wires and write "fuck you" with lipstick on the wind shield. He doesn't come home that night.

There are days I think if I forgive them then things will get back to normal. Whatever normal is. I am walking down to her house to talk it out she doesn't want to let me in. She says, "I'm busy." Ed tells me later that he was hiding in the other room. I just don't know what to do. I have been sitting in the dark living room for so many nights crying trying to figure out what is happening to my life. I know I need him to leave but haven't done it yet.

A few days later Ed and I have switched cars so he could go to a basketball game. Underneath the seat, I find a very descriptive letter. I read what she has written him about how much she cares and wants to be with him always. I have just gotten to Mom's house with the kids for dinner. I don't stay long. I'm trying to get my head around all of this. It is dark outside and I have packed his things including my wedding ring in a box. I hear him drive up. I am standing in the kitchen doorway as he walks in. He picks up the box and leaves. Nothing is said. He knows it's time.

I filed for divorce. Ed has been gone for about six months and it seems like the right time. Ed went to live with this woman for a week or so but didn't like it and is living by himself in a rented room. Her husband has left her. Ed comes over to see the kids most weekends and I let him stay. We don't even explain to the kids what is going on they are to young. I go to work for the first time in our married life. I am working at Liberty Carton filling in for a woman who is on maternity leave. They promise me I will have a job when she comes back. I am only there for six months when she comes back they give me a secretary position even though they know I can't type. They fire me after a week. But for the first time in the ten years I have been married I have my own money and am doing pretty well. I clear eighty one dollars a week and, although Ed is paying the house payment, I am doing the rest and manage to take the kids to McDonalds once a week. The kids are six and a half and eight and a half and come home from school to an empty house. The one thing I can't afford is a babysitter during the day. They call me to let me know they are home but they are on their own.

Beth has a little cut on her forehead. I realize it needs to be seen by a doctor but I also know I can't take time off work. She can walk to our doctor on her way home from school, the office is a block from our house, but can I let her do this by herself? She is only six and a half. Against my better judgment, I send her by herself. She has a little vein that has popped and needs to be cauterized. The doctor calls me and says, "She needs a really big treat. She was very good." She has done this on her own at six and a half years old. I feel so guilty.

Beth needs to go to the doctor again but I take her. She is getting nose bleeds and I can't figure it out. He looks at me and says, "Well, if you weren't pulling her pigtails so tight she'd be fine." I am pulling her hair so tight to get it perfect that I am breaking the blood vessels in her nose. I think if the house is perfect and the kids are perfect then our life would be perfect. It isn't.

We are still separated and I have made an appointment with a Rabbi. If Ed and I aren't together, I know I can't raise the kids Catholic. But could I raise them Jewish? I am getting ready to leave. It is snowing. It's a huge snow storm, so I cancel my appointment. I never make another one.

Ed is still drinking and has another car accident. He's totaled our car and tried to run away from the scene. I get the call. No one is hurt, thank God, but it could have been terrible. This time I go to his dad for the money to get him out of jail. As I walk up to the door, his father answers and says, "My mother is visiting and I don't want her to know what is going on." He closes the door. I am standing there all by myself shocked, scared and mad as hell. I call my dad again and he gives me the money to get Ed out of jail. I am driving Ed home and we are heading for Ed's rented room and he says, "Aren't I going to the house?" For the first time, I say to Ed, "This is your bag, baby, you live with it."

Ed has to go to court. They tell him either thirty days in jail or thirty days in treatment for alcoholism. He chooses treatment.

Ed is in Golden Valley Treatment Center for a one month inpatients treatment. I am resolved that this marriage is over. He calls after being there for about two weeks. He says, "The affair is finally over, and since I am Catholic and I have no idea how I feel about my religion would you hold off on the divorce until I can sort things out?" He also says, "I don't want to lose my family." I have no idea why I believe him and say, "Yes."

"Where's Daddy?" the kids ask. I tried to explain that daddy is getting help and could not drink anymore. It's Easter Sunday. Ed calls and asks if we will come have breakfast with him at the center. Beth, who is seven, sees Ed putting milk, juice and coffee on his tray. She pulls on my shirt and says "I thought you said Daddy couldn't drink anymore." I burst out laughing. I guess I didn't explain it very well.

A New Life

Ed starts going to Alcoholic Anonymous (AA) and I start going to Al-anon. It is the first time in my life that I know I have a choice, that if I don't like something I can do something about it. Even though I have made other choices, like leaving Germany earlier then Ed and knowing it was time to pack his things and have him leave these felt like reactions not choices. Can I deal with the fear? Can I start to feel better about myself? At least now, I feel I have a chance.

Its Friday night and Ed is still in treatment. We are going to an open AA meeting. An open meeting is a speaker meeting. Someone gets up and tells their story. These are the only meetings we can go to together. The others are separate. AA is for the person that drinks and Al-anon is for family members. It is a whole new life for us. Ed says, "I love my family and want us to stay together. Family means everything to me." I feel the same way. He says, "I finally know what is wrong and I'm going to do something about it." It is 1973. I am thirty years old.

I have gotten another job at Kirsch fabric. I am doing inventory control for the warehouse. I meet Barb at this job; she is eighteen. We have lunch together every day and I talk a lot about Al-Anon. She isn't sure if her father has a problem and asks to go to a meeting with me. I get fired from that job also. But I am beginning to take responsibility for my own behavior and realize that one of the reasons I get fired is my mom is in the hospital and I leave work early almost every day to go see her. Before Al-anon I would have blamed everyone except myself for everything. Ed and I are at a meeting and someone asks me what I do. I say, I'm not working right now." Ed looks at me and says, "This is an honest program, tell them what happened." This honesty thing is new for us. I tell them I have gotten fired that day. It's not easy growing up sometimes. But it is always good.

We have been separated for nine months. Ed wants an answer whether he can come home or not. I tell him, "I am going to Chicago to Phyllis's wedding I'll give you an answer when I get home." I tell him yes the next week.

Although Naomi and I have been getting along, she calls she says, "Will you go to counseling with me?" I'm surprised but agree because I'm thinking maybe with all the help I'm getting our relationship can get better also. We are walking into the counselor office, She says, "Please sit down and get comfortable" As we settle in Naomi turned to me and says, "I have been resentful of you all my life." I look at her shocked and say, "I'm thirty years old. I'm not going anywhere. Get over it." I find a voice and it feels wonderful. I'm done taking the blame for how she feels.

A New Ed

After a few months I begin to see the person I have always wanted emerge in Ed. My prince. He is kind and loving and happy to be with us. It is a new experience for me to be happy and smiling and feeling good. All of a sudden we talk about everything. How we feel, what we want to do over the weekend, simple things and hard things . We never talked like this before and it is new and different and exciting. We are making decisions together. We are more affectionate with each other and I begin to trust him. He is making new friends but also running into some of the people we used to drink with, even some he had gone to high school with that are in the program. He feels energized and alive. So do I.

He is going to speak and tell his story this Friday night at a meeting. He calls my Dad and says, "I would like you to come hear my story at the AA meeting Friday night." We are sitting in the meeting. Ed is up front telling his story. Dad has tears in his eyes. I don't think Dad ever looks at Ed the same way again. They always seemed to like each other but Dad was angry at Ed's behavior until this point. Mom is pretty sick now and although she knows Ed is getting better she is wrapped up in her own illness and can't really see beyond that. She is not well enough to come to a meeting. Dad says to Ed, "Thank you for letting me come."

New Beliefs

I am still having a lot of trouble believing in GOD and GOD as a higher power is a huge part of the program. I'm with Dad and ask, "How do you feel about GOD?" He says, "Both mother and I are atheists." Do I have trouble because if I believe in GOD is that going against them? Over the next few months my higher Power becomes my group and my friends and AA and Al-anon became a spiritual place for us and I understand for the first time it is different than religion.

Before Al-Anon I was so wrapped up in trying to keep a perfect house and make a perfect life that the kids got pushed to the side. It was more important to me that they looked good, that the house looked good than to talk about their feeling. It was what I learned in my family. Don't talk about things. If you don't, maybe they will go away.

Now that we are in AA and Al-Anon, one of the first things I am told is that if you get better the kids will follow. I'm not sure that actually happens unless you give them the attention they need which I didn't do.

We have started a family class about "Unspoken Rules". This is an expectation we have that we never speak about or tell the other person about. We just think they should know what we want. In class I am learning that although I haven't said it out loud I expect Ed to always kiss me hello and goodbye every day. When I tell him this out loud he doesn't have a clue and laughed and says, "That's not a problem."

Beth has been waking us up every weekend morning running into our room as soon as she wakes up. We try and try to explain to her that we want to sleep a little longer that she can go watch TV until we get up. Beth tells us her unspoken rule, "When I'm up everyone in the house should be up." Once it is said out loud she never wakes us up again.

Things really seem to be going our way for a change. I finally stop blaming others for what's happening to me. I learn to ask questions, like the time I ask the group, "What is an unfounded fear?" I explain that Ed is now sober and doing so well but I am still so afraid of his driving. Betty says, "Unfounded fear, hell, he's a horse shit driver" We all laugh until we hurt.

We have stopped seeing most of our drinking friends but hang with Anita and Bob and have stopped going to parties with the neighbors. We are at Anita's. She offers me a drink. I say, "No thanks." As we walk home Ed says, "Don't you ever turn down a drink when you want one. I am the alcoholic, not you" I stop worrying that he will drink again.

Three Weeks of Heaven

We have been in the program for about a year now. Mom is still not doing well. She has had her leg amputated five inches below the knee because of the diabetes and can't go to Puerto Rico with Dad. He asks if I want to go. Ed agrees it is a good idea and is willing to stay alone with the kids, which is new for him. I will be gone for three weeks.

I finally see my father in his own element. We are staying at the Caribe Hilton Hotel and it is beautiful. The ocean and beach are right outside. Dad has rehearsals most days and concerts most nights. I am sitting at a rehearsal and it is amazing. To see these artists I have heard about all my life actually there and my dad is with them. I begin to understand who he is and what he feels. I go to the beach at least a couple hours every day and I'm getting tan. I love to be tan. I feel healthy. Most nights after the concerts, Dad and some of the other guys go gambling. They love to play craps. I have never seen anything as exciting as Dad, Itzah Perlman and Alexander Schneider shooting craps. They are screaming and yelling and having a ball. I give Dad five dollars every night to play for me and each morning he gives me back twenty five. It took me years to realize he just gave me twenty five even if I didn't win. Dad and I are sitting on a couch outside the casino waiting for his friends. I am wearing a black halter top with wide bell bottom pants and my best jewelry. We have just come from a concert. A very good looking man comes up to us and asks if I would like to go have a drink with him. I look at Dad then look up at this very handsome man and say, "I'm sorry I don't think my husband would approve." It is the first time, I feel attractive. Then I try to baby-sit dad, "How much did you lose?" I ask. Not So Smart. Dad says, "You don't need to take care of me. I am an adult and know what I am doing." I finally understand.

Dad and Mom went to Puerto Rico for twenty three years. It was his time of glory, his special time to be exactly who he was. I don't think I ever saw him as happy as he was playing craps or playing his violin. The worst was the one year he won a lot and when he went to get it out of the box someone had stolen it all. They knew it was an employee of the hotel but couldn't prove it.

The only letter I got from Ed says, "where in the hells the sugar." I laughed out load.

I am coming off the airplane after three weeks. Ed is there to pick us up. He doesn't seem very excited to see me. I begin to worry. I'm a worrier. I have everything spread out unpacking on the living room floor and say to him, "Aren't you glad to see me?" His says, "You are so tan, that when you got off the plane all I could see were your eyes and your teeth. You don't look like you." We just laughed.

New Thoughts

Have you ever felt like a petulant child one minute, stomping your feet and wanting what you want right now? And in the next breath wondering if it is OK to ask for what you need? I am learning what that means in Al-Anon. What do I want? What do I need? These are hard questions for me to answer. I'm not sure I am looking deep enough into my life. But I sure want to.

Old Stuff to Deal With

I have not seen Judy for quite a long time. She married her high school sweetheart and Ed and I were in the middle of alcoholism. I have been in Al-anon for about a year learning that If I deal honestly with certain issues that have happened in my life the negative feeling around it can go away. I have to deal with the eighth grade issue around the Jewish group. I am still pretty confused about what happened and how I reacted to it. I had cut myself off. Why? Why hadn't I just told them to go to hell and continue on with my life? What is my part in this?

I call Judy and ask if we can talk. I ask, "Can you help me with my questions? I'm in Al-Anon now and learning so much but need help." We are sitting facing each other on the stools in her kitchen I ask the questions that have been plaguing me for years. "Do you remember the event? What is your memory of it?" She doesn't remember anything about it and never understood why I had gone away. She says, "Knowing the kind of person I am, do you think I was there?" As we talk we realize the girl that set the meeting up didn't invite Judy because she knew Judy wouldn't have let it happen. We talk for over three hours.

I also know now that it was my choice to leave the Jewish group. It was a choice I made because I didn't know how to speak up or deal with what was happening. I had to stop blaming everyone else. Judy has so much courage. I think she was the conscious of our little group when we were kids. She truly has a voice.

As our day is ending we know we want to keep seeing each other, we don't want to lose track again. She says, "Let's meet once a year in October for lunch after the kids go back to school." On our first lunch, we start catching up. We have so much to tell each other, it's a little scattered. She says, "Why don't we each take an hour and share what is going on in our lives. Then we can talk about life etc after?" We end up talking together for hours. During the next year, I read in the paper that Judy's father has died. It's not time for our lunch but I know I need to be there and see her. I go to the shiva. Shiva is a Jewish tradition a little bit like a wake where people come to pay their respects to the family. It can last up to seven days all day and evening. I am walking in. Judy starts to cry and hugs me hard surprised I am there but glad to see me. She says, "Oh you came." I say, "Of course I'm here."

Its about six months later and I am waiting for Reva, Judy's mom to come to the restaurant. I want to ask her what she remembers about my parents, sister and my family. Reva says, "I have known your parents for a long time." She says, "Your parents are considered intellects and rich and people don't understand them." She says, "My brother is a communist," and she tells me about him and about her understanding about this kind of politics and that her husband didn't want the kids to have any part of it and that is why he didn't want Judy going to the picnics with me. I'm not ready to hear about politics yet so I tune her out. She tells me she understands how difficult it is with my sister. The fact that Naomi had gotten married so young and had a baby at sixteen was the talk of the neighborhood and Reva heard it all. So between politics and Naomi, no wonder I am confused about how all this played out in my family and my life.

It is time for me to understand more of where I came from so I can understand where I want to go. I have a part in what is happening to me. What is it? What will I learn? How much of a role does the fear play in all of this?

Where is politics in all this? I know at this point I don't want anything to do with it. Politics still scars me to death. But Al-Anon and conversations like the one I had with Judy and Reva help me to understand more and more.

1981 Not a Good Year

I am over at the big house seeing dad. He says, "They sent me these papers about resuscitating Mom or not when the time came." I say," You know she is not going to get better? You need to sign the papers saying do not resuscitate." In a tiny voice he says, " Can't you sign? I can't." I can understand how he feels. Their relationship is very much like mine and Ed's when Ed was drinking. Dad is the enabler/caretaker and Mom's behavior is very much like Ed's when he drinks. Mom is very controlling and angry and Dad thinks his job is to keep things calm. Just like I do. He finally agrees to sign the papers never believing it will come to that. The diabetes is taking its toll. Mom came home a few years ago from Puerto Rico with a black toe. I noticed it when I go see her. She had not noticed it. She had the first surgery to remove the toe, Her second surgery a few years after that was to remove the foot and the third, when I went to Puerto Rico amputating her leg five inches below the knee. Again she has to figure out how to live with this and she does. The day she gets out of the hospital she gets herself a cab and goes to get her hair and nails done. For the next eight years she never stops living her life. We come over to see her and she calls to one of the kids, "Go get my leg." It became part of all of us. She has lost her eye sight and now a leg but as amazing as she is, it is taking a toll.

For many years she has used the diabetes to control everything in her life. They say in Al-anon that diabetes is much like alcoholism.

While alcoholism is emotional, physical and spiritual, diabetes is emotional and physical. It's not always easy being around her. Her anger has gotten worse. My dad has become the caretaker and allowing her to get away with nasty behavior. Yet who can blame her. She has lost so much. First her eyesight, now her leg.

Since I have gone back to work I have not been able to give her the time she needs like I had done all the years I had my grandfather's car. Actually, it feels like our roles have reversed. I feel like the mom taking care of the child. Yet, I stop at their house every day after work to talk or just to see her. When Ed was still drinking, I would stop to complain. Now its just to see her.

My parents built an apartment on the back of their house for my grandmother after my grandfather died. As my mother gets sicker, my grandmother takes over my mom's role in her own house, planning and cooking dinners and running the household. I know my grandmother is doing what she thinks is best but she is taking my mother's place away. Mom has given up. She goes upstairs to her room at dinner time and reads or meditates while my grandmother takes over the kitchen, all the while complaining that she is tired and really doesn't want to do this anymore but she doesn't know how to stop.

Naomi and I have decided to have a surprise forty fifth wedding anniversary party for Mom and Dad. We realize Mom will probably not make 50th. Aunt Lottie has still never accepted Ed being he is Catholic and all. We have invited people from all over. All of Mom

What a Party

and Dad's friends are coming. Ed has just gotten home from picking up Lottie and Sam at the airport and taking them to their hotel settling them in. He says, "Lottie was very nice," which surprises us. We are all gathered in Naomi's back yard. Lottie is saying to everyone, "That Ed, he's such a doll." Mom and Dad are walking in. They are totally surprised and a bit overwhelmed. It is everything we want it to be. I start to cry.

Mom's bones are so brittle she broke her hip by just lifting herself off the couch onto the floor to do her exercises. She is in the hospital. She getting more and more discouraged, not understanding why I am not there and why I can't do what she wants of me. With two kids and a job, I just don't have the time or the strength. Ed is getting a little irritated that I stop at Mom's so much. He doesn't understand why I have to see her everyday. His family is not like that.

Al-Anon has taught me a lot but I am really scared. I don't want to hurt her. Our relationship has improved over the years but it's still tenuous. I have grown up and understand what her life has been like. I also don't want her to get mad at me. I hate it when any one is mad at me.

Dad and I are on the way to the hospital to talk with her. We are sitting by her bedside. I'm nervous but say, "I love you so much but I just can't do everything. I need to take care of my family too. I want you to get better and to be around a long time."

We talk and talk and she hears every word I say about having a family of my own and that I really need to be more available to them. She says, "I totally understand." It feels good to speak my truth to Mom. She finally says, "I'm really tired and need to rest." That is the last time we talk. Roz called to say she had been to see Mom. She says, "Your mom turned her mind off." Roz is a regular visitor and one of Mom's best friends. She says, "Your mom isn't here anymore. She has so much pain in her life, she basically has left us with her mind." She has been in extended care off and on for eighteen months. Going home only to fall or break a bone and have to go back. The health care is running out. Dad has to put her in a nursing home.

Although the nursing home is a nice place, she is in the locked section because she isn't capable of taking care of herself any longer. She says to dad on one of his visits "What's wrong? Can't you afford to keep me in the hospital any longer?" She doesn't understand how hard it is on him that he had to take her out of the hospital and put her in a nursing home because Insurance wouldn't pay for the hospital any longer. He calls me in the evening and says, "Will you go with to see Mom? I can't go alone. I can't stand seeing her like this." She has been there for eight weeks. We have celebrated her birthday with her, and I have visited her weekly with dad she is now back in the hospital.

It's May 11, 1981. I am thirty seven years old. I'm leaving work early to go see Mom in the hospital. I'm coming up to the entrance. I can't go in. Something stops me. I drive home fix dinner for my family while wondering why I couldn't go in. Dad calls to say he isn't feeling well. I say, "If you need me, no matter what time, call me. I'll come right over."

Ed and I have just gotten into bed and the phone rings. It's the hospital, "We are so sorry to tell you but your mother just passed away and we just couldn't call your father." I say, "I understand. I will go tell him." I call Naomi and we meet at their house. Naomi is waking up Grandma to tell her. Ed and I are on our way upstairs to tell Dad.

He is just getting out of bed to call me, he says, "I think I am having a heart attack." Ed and I piled him into the car and raced to Methodist hospital. I am running up to the emergency room desk yelling, "Please help. My mother died upstairs an hour ago, my dad is in the car having a heart attack." Did they move! He was admitted. It turned out to be complete exhaustion. At this point, I haven't even had time to realize my mother is dead. I think he knew that night that she was going to die and that's why he got so sick. I know how he felt. I had gone to see my mother every day in the hospital that last week but the day she died something told me not to go in.

Dad has been in the hospital for about a week and can't go to the funeral. He hasn't been able to deal with the fact that she died.

I'm in bed and it's just after we got home from admitting Dad to the hospital when I feel this presence and I know deep down that it is Mom. I can tell she is in the room. The energy and feeling of comfort is amazing and shocking. I look up at the ceiling of our bedroom and whisper, "Goodnight Mom." I feel this every night.

Aunt Lottie

Aunt Lottie

It's only a few months since Mom died and Phyllis calls to say Uncle Morrie, Dad's brother, has been in a car accident. He broke his neck. He didn't survive. I'm at the big house talking to dad. He is so sad and says, "I can't go to Chicago. I can't do another funeral right now." Even though he didn't go to my mother's. He is not the same. He doesn't smile any more. Even though he is here, he is not here. He misses mom so much. We worry yet think that now he can start to do some of the things he has wanted to do like travel but couldn't because she was so sick. I call Phyllis back and say "I am coming and will see you as soon as I get there." Morrie was her dad. I adored

Morrie. He is the funny Uncle and loved kids. Phyllis is very close to Aunt Lottie. Aunt Lottie never had children and treats Phyllis like a daughter. If Lottie came to Minneapolis for anything she would bring Phyllis. Phyllis got divorced when the kids were little and she has two kids close in age to ours and brings them to Minneapolis every summer to see us. Our relationship has grown over the years and she loves Ed. They get along very well. We also adore her new husband, Skip.

Even though Aunt Lottie was great when they came for mom and dad's party when I walk into the Shiva for Morrie she doesn't talk to me. I have no idea why. I'm heading over to say hello and give her a hug. She says, "Why didn't you call me as soon as you got in?" I am surprised she is so angry. I say, "I went right to Phyllis house, I knew I would see you here tonight." She ignores me the rest of the time I'm there.

I'm home now and telling Dad what happened. I say, "I want to write her a letter telling her what I feel and how mean she was. Will you read it before I send it?" Dad says, "Do it." I write her everything I feel. I say, "I came to Chicago because my friend's father had died. Although I understand how hard this is for you, Phyllis was my priority." I tell her "I don't like being snubbed. I am a different person from the young girl who sent the pictures of me on the altar marrying Ed. I am a grown woman and have feelings just like everyone else and it is time you accepted that." Dad just finished reading the letter and says, "Mail it." Sure enough she calls him just furious. Dad tells me she yells at him on the phone "How ungrateful Leslie is and she had insulted me by not calling me first and rushing to my side." All he responds with is, "Read it again. It is a very good letter." I'm still having trouble telling someone how I feel to their face but writing it down always helps. I feel very good about how I handled this situation.

Dad

Over the next year, Dad spends many many days and nights with us. He calls in this little voice and says, "Hi." I say, "Want dinner?" He says, "Yes," and comes over. At dinner we laugh and my kids get to know him even more then they did already and love having him around. It's Sunday morning. He is over for breakfast. Greg says, "Please pass the salami." Dad picks up a piece and throws it at him. How could we not laugh at him?

"Dad, do you want to come live with us? We can build a room on the back of our house for you?" He says, "I can't do that." Then says, "We did that for Grandma and it didn't work out so well. My grandmother still lives in the apartment attached to mom and dad's house. I also don't want to intrude on your family." We tell him, "We love spending time with you and never feel you are intruding."

Dad has left to go see Aunt Lottie in Palm Springs and then on to New York to see his friends there. It is about a year since Mom died. I don't feel her presence any longer. I think she needed to go with him. We think the trip will be wonderful for him. He has been so sad since mom died. Maybe he can start living again.

After about a week he calls and says, "I'm not feeling well I'm coming home." His secretary picked him up at the airport and I'm at the big house talking to him. We are fighting. He just doesn't understand why I can't be friends with Aunt Lottie. I try to explain again. "I am finally finding out about myself and will not let anyone treat me that way any longer," I say. I leave in a huff and when I get home I tell Ed how mad I am, "Why doesn't he understand how hard this is for me?" I'm furious.

That night, Dad went out to dinner with my sister and her kids. The next morning he calls me, "Want to meet at the Lincoln Del for breakfast?" After we are sitting, he apologizes to me for the first time in my life. He says, "I understand, I just want you to like her and I feel bad that you can't get along."

We drive back to the big house in separate cars. He drives into the garage and as he walks into the house my father has a heart attack. I start screaming and yelling. I call 911 as my grandmother came out of her apartment to see what the fuss is. She sits on the couch with her hand over her mouth as tears ran down her face. The paramedics crack his chest and bring him back to life but he never regains consciousness. I call Ed "Get over here as fast as you can." He says, "I don't have a car" I say, "get one." Anita and Bob give him theirs.

I am at the hospital every day. I know he isn't awake but I know he hears me. I talk to him, I say, "Well Pop, I have to go home and feed the kids," and he moans. No matter what I talk to him about he moans at the right moment. He is on a respirator and Naomi and I know he hates it. He always said, "I just want to have a heart attack one day and be gone," and here he is lying in a hospital bed hooked up to all these machines.

Naomi and I are walking down the hall to the doctor's office. When we get there we say, "Please take him off the respirator, he's not going to live." The next morning we are in dad's room and the doctor shuts the machines off and takes them away. We ask, "What happens now?" "Within twenty four to forty eight hours his temperature will get so high it will shut down his organs." It doesn't happen. We ask why? They say, "His temperature hasn't risen because we are giving him Tylenol rectally." The doctor is a friend of dad's and he says, "I don't want to lose him. This is so hard." We say, "PLEASE let him go." One year and one week after my mom died, dad dies on his seventy second birthday. He had been so excited about getting social security that month. He had still been working and didn't know he could get Social Security sooner. We had to send the first check back because he didn't live the whole month.

It's a couple months after dad is gone. I get a call from the Social Security office asking, "Are you related to Theodore Ptashne?" "Well," they say, "if you send us the death certificate we have about twelve thousand dollars that was owed your dad." He didn't realize he could have been collecting for both him and my mom. Naomi and I split it when the check comes. I know he loves it. I feel his presence the night he dies but push him away. I am angry that I am not enough to keep him alive. I am devastated. I know my heart had been broken once before when I found out about the affair. This felt the same.

Naomi and I were walking through the house knowing everything had to be sold. As we look at the things we want to take and as we divide up the contents of Mom and Dad's life, we talk for the first time in a long time. "Although these things are important, they are not as important as our relationship," she says. I agree. No material thing is worth getting in between us. I wish that feeling could have lasted. Later I realize he wants me to have a relationship with Aunt Lottie because he knew he was dying and didn't want me to be alone.

Grandma

It's two months after dad died. My grandmother is in the hospital. She is ninety two years old saying, "Why am I still here?" I ask my grandmother for money.

I am going to Winona, MN with my niece Sandy and Beth. Phyllis and her daughter Stacy are driving from Chicago to see the campus because Stacy is going there to college. I don't have any money to go and still don't want to ask Ed.

It's Saturday morning in the motel. I wake up with this very strange feeling that is hard to explain or even identify but I am unsettled and jittery. I ask Phyllis, "Can you take the girls with you? I just want go to the pool by myself." She says, "Yes." I am lying by the pool. I look up in to the sky for no apparent reason and say, "Bye Gram, I love you." At dinner I say to Phyllis, "I think my grandmother died today." I have just gotten home and as I walk into the living room I say to Ed, "What time did my grandmother die yesterday?" He says, "How did you know?" "I don't know. I just knew."

In fourteen months they are all gone. My mom, my dad and my grandmother. I have no regrets with my mom or my dad. I had done everything I could. We spent so much time with Dad and had such a good time that last year. I do have regrets with my grandmother. I had been so proud of myself for not taking money from my grandparents when I was a teenager. When we got married and Ed was drinking,

I went back on my values and because we didn't have any money I started to ask for help. I know I disappointed them and me. After a few years in AA and Al-Anon, Ed and I make a conscious decision to never ask for money we couldn't pay back.

My Dad has loaned us money for a car. I have made a payment schedule and am paying him every month. He is over for dinner. It's after mom has died. He says, "Can I see that schedule for the car payments? I just want to see how much is left." I hand it to him and he rips it up. Grandma has loaned us money for the siding on the addition we were putting on the house. We paid it off completely with interest and all. We feel so good about ourselves and how much we have changed and how far we have come. Now I have to deal with being the last entry in her checkbook. Although I can't do anything about it, I vow I will never ask anyone for money again. If I don't have my own, I either don't go or don't get it.

In fourteen months they are all gone, I miss them everyday.

The House of Note

We have been trying to sell the House of Note dad's violin shop for the last year. Ed just walked in from work, he says, "I have a buyer for the shop." "Really? Who?" "ME!" "What!!!" Ed tells me, "I talked with Tom today and he reminded me that I have always wanted a business of my own and I'm sitting on one." Ed tells Tom, "I don't know anything about violins," Tom's answer is, "You will learn." Ed has never been without a job, even through the drinking years. He has been selling various things at various jobs but never liking it. We don't have any money but he works hard. We call Naomi and say, "We would like to buy your half of the shop." She agrees. It is 1983 and Ed steps in to take over. It is not a very thriving business and there is a lot of work to do. Ed sends Naomi a check every month for her half of the business. He is working six days a week and learning so much. I have been helping out for a couple months. I am sitting at the desk balancing the check book. Ed is standing over my shoulder making sure I'm doing everything right. It's very annoying. He has been standing over my shoulder every day that I come in. I turn around and say, "If you want me to do anything, bring it home. I'm done." I pick up my purse and walk out. He brings the checkbook home every month for me to balance. It works out much better and he knows it too.

Making Up with Aunt Lottie

Its 1983, a year since Dad has been gone and because of the fight we had about being friends with Aunt Lottie, I think I will try patch things up and go see her. They have a home in Palm Springs and live there in the winter. Aunt Lottie's favorite color is apricot. In their apartment in Chicago they have a hand woven apricot rug with a design etched out in the middle. It is gorgeous. In Palm Springs, they bought the model home and everything is apricot, silver and glass.

I am standing at the kitchen sink in Palm Springs helping Aunt Lottie with the dishes. She says, "I will never understand how you could have sent those pictures of you kneeling at the altar to your grandmother." My stomach starts turning upside down as I quickly try to figure out what to say. I answer "You know that was a very long time ago, how about we just forget it?" Nothing more is said.

Its 1986, Phyllis and I are in Palm Springs we have started coming here together every March. We are on our way to The Hilton Hotel for Rack of Lamb before 5:00 pm because it is cheaper. Tomorrow I'm sure we will go to The Chinese restaurant and the next night the Delicatessen. Every time we come we go to the same places.

Phyllis and I are getting ready for bed and saying good night to Aunt Lottie and Uncle Sam. Lottie hands us each an envelope. We get into the bedroom and open the envelopes. We can't believe what we see. There is a check for fifteen thousand dollars in each of our en-

Phyllis and Me

velopes. We almost have a heart attack! What a blessing. I don't think I have ever seen this much money in one check. Aunt Lottie gives us each a check ever time we come for the next five years. It is helping me learn how to deal with money a little better. I gave Ed ten thousand dollars from the first check for the violin shop and bought us a new bedroom set that we really needed. The next few years I learn to save not only spend what I have.

I have just gotten a call from Phyllis. Sam is in the hospital and the woman that is watching Aunt Lottie, who now has Alzheimer's, is abusing her. Phyllis can't go. I get the next flight out. Phyllis has set up meetings with some caregiver to interview. Sam just got home from the hospital and we are sitting at the dining room table and talking. I ask, "What can I do to help? I think it is the first time Sam sees that I am only there to help and nothing more. I have always felt he didn't like us and thought we were there only for the money. Our relationship after that was very good. Lottie died in Chicago at the age of ninety four. Uncle Sam had died the year before. I feel I have made peace with them.

My Wonderful Job

Its 1988, I have never had a job I liked although I have had several. Ed is doing something he likes and learning so much yet I still feel stuck. I'm not enjoying our life and I'm not sure why. Barb called today crying. "Do you remember me?" and says "I think I married one." She starts Al-anon the next week. I have been going to a different group and a couple weeks later one of the gals says, "We have a job opening at my office. Anyone interested?" I jumped on it. I applied for the job and got it.

I am sitting on a bench outside the office of the Pilling Pain clinic at Fairview Southdale Hospital. I have gotten the job as the administrative assistant. I am waiting for Mark my boss to come get me and start teaching me what I need to know and do. As I learn this job, I realize I have finally found something that I love to do. Mark has the best sense of humor and I am learning to laugh again. I haven't laughed in a long time. My desk is in the front so I am the first person anyone sees as they walk into the clinic. Mark comes in, it's first thing in the morning. He has the paper and a muffin and tells me, "I'll be back soon." We both know where he is going and laugh. I stay at this job for six years and learn so much about myself. I learn I am capable and smart. I get along with the other staff and we help each other out.

Quitting at Last

Ed's dad is pressuring Ed's mom to quit smoking. Lila always says, "I can quit anytime I want, I just don't want to. But I will show everyone that I can do it for ONE YEAR and ONE YEAR only. I decide to quit with her.

I have heard about many different things that will help me quit. There is the patch, a plastic patch with medicine in it that you put on your skin to stop the cravings. I know from taking some prescriptions drugs and the reaction I get from the side effects that they don't work for me. So I don't want to do that. Then there is hypnotism but I don't think it will work on me; you have to relax and I don't do that well. So I say no to that also. A friend has mentioned acupuncture. I think this might work. I look up a clinic in the yellow pages and make an appointment for both Lila and myself. Acupuncture is the first time I try alternative medicine. I think what the heck let's try this and see what happens.

It's a week after my first treatment and I'm down to the basement digging for butts in the garbage. I call them and say, "I need another treatment or I'll smoke." I have the second treatment and I never smoke again. Ed has already quit and says, "This is as hard on me as it is on you." All the emotions that I have held in for years are flying out. I am so angry with Ed and I'm not sure why. We're doing pretty good, why now? Maybe I have never really expressed all the feelings I have from the drinking years. I'm not sure. All I know right now is I'm angry as hell at Ed. All he has to do is ask me a question and I jump all over him. We are standing in the kitchen and he asks, "What's for dinner?" "What difference does it make? It's just dinner." I answer. I barely say hello when he comes in from work. My anger is at the edge and for the first time I understand addiction. Smoking is an addiction. Mine!

I have changed where I sit at the kitchen table reading the paper because if I sit in my regular spot I want a cigarette. When I clean the house after each room I would sit down and have a cigarette at the kitchen table. I realize that cigarettes are my way to relax. My justification is life has been hard who wouldn't need to relax.

It's been about two weeks. My emotions are so raw I come into work every morning and if anyone so much as talks to me, even saying hello I burst into tears. I hadn't felt the feeling I am feeling in a very long time. I feel sad, overwhelmed and lonely. Maybe even though I have felt these I have never acknowledged them. Mark says, "Go into the bathroom and get yourself together," with a smile. "I'll watch the front desk." I don't know what to do with this kind of support.

Ed and I are celebrating our twenty fifth wedding anniversary. We always go out to dinner with Anita and Bob because their anniversary is a few days before ours.

We just walked in the house and there is a party going on. Unbeknownst to us, Beth planned a surprise party. Phyllis and Skip have come from Chicago. And most of our friends and relatives are here. Beth has collected money for a gift certificate at a travel agency.

My nieces and nephews all six of them aren't here. The next day I call Naomi, "I missed the kids. I wish they could have been at the party." My niece calls a couple days later. She is yelling at me saying, "Just because you have given us presents for our birthday doesn't mean we have to come and give you one for your anniversary." "What are you talking about?" I ask. "All I said was I missed you." She won't listen to me. She is screaming and screaming that I have no right to expect them to give me presents. I can't believe what I am hearing. It has been such a good weekend celebrating with Phyllis and Skip. They drove up from Chicago just for the party and to spend the weekend with us. It has made it very special. So I have no idea where this screaming and yelling is coming from. Shaking with anger, I scream back, "FUCK YOU" and hang up. WOW! Where did that come from? It feels really, really good. Naomi calls a week later saying, "My family and I have decided to start celebrating birthdays and holidays alone with just our immediate family." I realize this is the consequence for speaking up. My family is getting smaller and smaller. Years later, Naomi called and asked me why we didn't get together as a family any longer. I told her that had been her decision and I was honoring it. She didn't remember what had happened.

It's one year later to the day that Lila and I quit smoking. Lila calls and says, "Are you going to start smoking today?" I am stunned. "I don't want to go through that ever again," I say. She says, "I have proven to everyone that I can quit anytime I want to. So I'm going to start again today." I don't think I have known anyone who loves to smoke as much as Lila does. Except maybe my dad. He quit when mom was sick and couldn't smoke in the house anymore.

I have been dealing with quitting smoking and the huge fight with my niece and another separation from my sister. I have all this emotion right on the edge. Why would I want to go through this ever again.

Our First Trip

We have decided to use the gift from our anniversary to go to Glacier National Park. We think taking the train will be romantic and relaxing. We are on the train wondering why this feels like the longest trip in the world. Well, if we would have thought about where train tracks are and that trains go ten to fifteen miles an hour through every po-dunk town we might have made a different decision. We have arrived in White Fish and are talking with the hotel clerk trying to get a one-way flight for when we go home but it's just too expensive.

Before we leave I say to Ed, "Don't you think we need hiking boots?" "No, our tennis shoes will be fine." The first day is muddy and wet; our shoes are ruined. We are in town trying to find a store that sells hiking boots, there is one store and the only ones they have in our size are the most expensive, of course. We just laugh.

A friend has told me to be sure to go to Hidden Lake. She says, "It is the most beautiful thing I've ever seen." It's at the end of the hiking path of the Sun Road. We are hiking the sun road. I see a big horned sheep right next to us. We are at the end; the lake is completely covered in fog. I pull up my jacket hood and take a picture to show her. Hidden Lake is hidden.

We decide to go White Water Rafting. What a blast! We have on life jackets tightened so tight I can hardly breathe, so no matter what we won't drown. How encouraging. We get into the raft and as we head down the river the water is spraying us. It is really cold. What a wild ride. As the white rapids hit the raft we bounce up, down and sideways holding on for dear life. When we get done we can't unbutton our life vests because our hands are just about frozen. We love every minute of it. We are hiking up a mountain to take pictures at the top. I realized in that moment I am happy and happy with Ed. We are completely relaxed and truly enjoying each other. We talk to each other about what we want to do each day. We are laughing a lot and I feel connected to Ed for the first time in ages. Something different has happened as we travel together and I want more.

What Now?

I feel like I'm going crazy. Ed and I are in bed. I wake up at 6:30 am
or so and Ed is snoring softly beside me. I can't stand him. I want to
kill him and he hasn't even opened his eyes yet. It takes me several
months to put these feelings together with when I am getting my
period. Once I do, I start marking it on the calendar and tell Ed,
"Look out the week has started." The kids are on their own now,
Greg away at college and Beth living and working on her own. At
least they don't have to feel the brunt of this. Pre-menopause; I had
no idea what that was. I have about thirteen hot flashes a day and
overwhelming emotions. It's not the quitting smoking any longer.
That's been awhile but now it's happening again. On with the sweater,
off with the sweater. Layers and layers of clothes on in the winter
but no wool it make me itch. After about six months of this I call my
doctor and say, "Am I going crazy?" NOPE! He starts me on a natural
progesterone/estrogen cream. I put it on my underarms and thighs
every day, twice a day. I never forgot to put it on. The hot flashes go
away and moods calm down. I can like Ed again.

Running

Ever since we have gotten back from our trip things have gone back to the way they were. Ed is quiet and distance. How can things change so quickly? The trip was so wonderful and then we are home...

Ed has been running for about a year. He started running when he quit smoking. What a change for him. New business and now exercise. I am surprised but glad that he is doing this. After I quit smoking, I think why not I'll start running too. I am forty five years old. I start with one block. I don't tell Ed. I want to be able to run a whole mile first. What if I can't do it, then if I have told him will he be disappointed in me. I say to Ed, "I have started running maybe it is something we will have in common." He is much faster than I am and has joined a health club and has made new friends. He tells me, "I don't want you to meet them. You tend to take over in a group and this is my group and I want to keep them separate. It is the first time I feel like I really belong someplace that you're not a part of." I am so sad but what can I do but honor his feelings.

I can't seem to catch my breath while I'm running. I decide to go to the doctor and after a lot of tests I am diagnosed with exercise-induced asthma. The doctor has put me on an inhaler and although I don't like taking prescription drugs of any kind it does help. I decide to join the club. I have met a new friend. We run together every morning. Ed runs in the evenings after work so we don't meet up with each other. Here we are together but separate. He and his friends decide to do a marathon. Training for a marathon takes a lot of time. Ed is running every day sometimes ten to twenty miles with his friends. He tells me, "Jan and I share a lot with each other. It is really nice and we have become really good friends." I feel like we are back in old territory and I am jealous. I want Ed to want me as his best friend. I'm not speaking up and he has a crush. I am still afraid to say what I feel. I don't think Ed will understand why I am upset. He is sober, has friends of his own for the first time in a long time and I do know he would never have another affair so why do I even think that. Ed has just come home from running. He has been out by himself. He does that some times and says, "Remember when I told you about the big sale at the shop?" I say, "You never told me that." He is confused; he is sure he did. I ask, "Were you thinking about this when you were running? Maybe you thought you told me but didn't." Something has changed. Ed is not talking to me as much about what is going on with him. I don't know his feelings right now. I try to handle my feelings around Ed by talking with my girlfriends. A lot of time it's just complaining about him while feeling hurt and sad. I'm still not sure what to do with hurt and sad. I don't know how to combat this so I keep quiet, too quiet. I am afraid to disagree with him because if I do he will get angry. It brings back instant memories of the drinking years. If he got mad at me drunk although he never hit me, there was a lot of blaming. I believed all the bad things he said about me. It also brings me back to being five years old and my sister is threatening to hit me or yelling at me telling me how terrible I am and what an awful person I am. I believed both of them and it has taken years and a lot of counseling to understand why I feel the way I do about myself but now it's all back and it doesn't feel good. So even though

I don't worry about him having another affair because I don't think he would do that sober, I feel left out and alone. Ed and his friends, Jan and Bob D., went on to train together for fifteen marathons.

Naomi

Life seems to be forever changing. Alone yet married, afraid to speak up but knowing I have to and not knowing how. Naomi and I have been getting along fairly well. Although we don't get together as a family, we have still been seeing each other once in a while. She has called and invited me out to lunch and as we sit visiting she says, "I have something to tell you." "I have done some counseling and I know Mother sexually abused me." I can't believe what I am hearing. How can she possibly believe that? I tell her, "It's not possible." If it happened to her, why had it not happened to me and I know it did not happen to me. I feel rage. She is accusing Mom when Mom isn't here any longer to defend herself. I tell Naomi my truth, "I don't believe it for a minute." I think about it later and realize she has been doing quite a bit of counseling and it is a time when many therapists are talking about repressed memories. Memories that we stuff way down because we don't want to remember them. I have no illusion that this is not true for Naomi. She may have been abused but I know without a shadow of a doubt it was not our mother. We have stopped talking. I can't give up who I am becoming for her any longer. I don't like what is happening. It is the first time I disagree with my sister and we stop talking to each other.

I am so conflicted. She is all I had left. Everyone else is gone. Is a bad relationship better than nothing? After not talking for about one and half years, Naomi calls and wants to go to lunch. We are sitting at the restaurant. I let her do most of the talking. I am still afraid to say everything I feel because I think if I do the relationship will fall apart again and I don't want that to happen. After that lunch if we see each other, we talk, get along and have fun together but we never talk about our parents. I miss that. I love remembering who they were and what they have given us. She doesn't want to mention them at all. It is still hard for me to claim my voice. I question things in my head and decide if it is worth speaking up or not. Most of the time it isn't, so I keep quiet. I'm not sure she would hear what I have to say anyway. Is that a justification because I am so afraid of conflict? I don't know.

I have been running since 1989 and Naomi started running a few years later. She calls, "Where are you going to be running on Saturday morning? I'll meet you there." She doesn't ask if it is OK to join me; she just assumes it is. It not OK. I begin to understand what Ed is feeling about me being in his group. Although I am glad we are speaking again, I know for my own self-preservation, I need to keep her at a distance. I can't be myself around her because there is so much we don't talk about. I am learning how important it is for me to speak my truth and I don't feel I can do that with her. She is pushing into my group trying to make friends with my friends and I don't want that.

We are in Palm Springs to see Aunt Lottie and we are out running. I finally say, "Why did you start running?" She says, "Because it would be something fun for sisters to do together." "You are absolutely right," I say, "it could be fun but you are doing to me what you have done to me all my life. You didn't ask me what I want." I say, "You will have to find a group of your own. I have my group and it is enough."

It is the second time I ever speak up to her. I'm not sure she heard me. I am on a committee for the Twin Cities Marathon. She gets on the Board. I work at Fairview Hospital. She gets a job at Fairview. Why is it so hard for me? Most people think if someone copies you it is a compliment. This is way beyond a compliment. This feels like an invasion into my life and I just don't want to deal with it. I am constantly flipping back and forth, strong and able to say what I need from her and being the frightened little sister that she was mean to.

I complain, crab and do everything but talk to her. This is such an old pattern. Why can't I say what I want to, to those I love.

I think about my fear. I think if I understand where it comes from it will go away. I wonder if Mom and Dad's politics has anything to do with it. I decided to do some research.

Politics and Religion Intermingled

I have not thought about politics or religion for a long time but start to wonder what it is all about. Going to Al-anon seems to take the place of both mine and Ed's religion. Ed has not gone to church for a long time. Yet when someone mentions GOD or Jesus, I get a tightening in my stomach. AA and Al-anon are based on a belief in a higher power. That something or some one greater then ourselves is in charge. Letting go and letting GOD is one of the sayings in the program. I am learning how to let go but not sure of the GOD thing. My parents were atheists so if I believe in GOD, am I going against them? I ask questions in meetings like, "How do you learn to believe in a Higher Power?" I think people who have had a formal religious upbringing understand the concept better. I have had no formal training in religion. I'm not sure where to start. I decide to call Mike, Dad's best friend. "Would you answer some questions for me about what my parents believed about their religion and politics?" He was involved with them from about 1947 until my dad died in 1982.

Mike and Roz are here and he asks me, "Why have you called this meeting?" I say "I want to understand where the changes came with my grandparents. Their parents were orthodox Jews in Russia, yet my grandparents had no formal religion at all." Neither did my parents. He talks a bit about the history for me of Judaism which helps put into perspective the issues I want to think about.

What I understand from the conversation is this: Way back at the beginning of time the prophets were politicians. They were trying to make a better world and to convince the people that their way was the best, whether it was Moses or Jesus. Mike tells me my grandparents were taught the way to live was to try and make a better world. The only education they had was in the Yiddish schools. There were two different sects in Russia: the Bund and the Yiddish. The Yiddish were the working or what we would call today the blue color group. The Bund were the wealth group. When my grandparents came here there were no Yiddish schools and the only way to follow through with what they believed was through politics. He also tells me that my parent's Higher Power was community and friends. I am feeling the same way. Asking these questions has helped. Mike has mailed me a few articles. One titled "Why Be Jewish." After I ask myself this question,

"WHY BE JEWISH"

For me being Jewish is a feeling of belonging to something even though I don't belong to a synagogue. It is a feeling that no matter where I go there are people that I can relate to about being Jewish. It is a feeling of being proud of something that I am and I am Jewish. It is something that I carry inside that is very hard for me to explain. It is hard to write out this feeling. It is so much a part of me that to not be Jewish would feel like I was losing a part of myself that helped make up the kind of person I have become. When Mike talked about the kind of life my parents tried to lead I know they taught me well, because I want the same things as they did. I know for me to be a kind, understanding, thoughtful person is what I am all about. To try and give love with no expectation that I must have something in return, is what I am working on. As I have been learning this past year, I have more feelings of calm than I ever have. It is not always a smooth road to get there but when I get there I feel better. When I start to stand up for myself and don't let people walk all over me I feel proud of myself. This is what kind of person I want to be and will continue to work towards that goal. I will not choose the same path that my parents took because politics is not my thing. But I think for me just working on being the kind of person I want to be is enough.

Writing this out helps me understand what my parents were all about and how much they have taught me. I am changing, learning, growing, and speaking up. Ed also feels the same way. We are in agreement that church or religion is not the way to go for us.

Beth is engaged to a Jewish man. We have raised our kids in the Catholic Church because Ed's folks being very religious said we had to or couldn't get married. We don't go to church much but they were both confirmed and both completed the required classes. When Beth was seven and it was time for her first confession Ed took her to church and she started crying and was so afraid he brought her home. He said, "No child of seven should have to be that scared."

It's Christmas 1994, Beth asks me to go with her to a meeting at Temple Israel Synagogue. It is called the December Dilemma. It is for interfaith couples that are engaged, married or just going together. Her fiancé has National Guard and doesn't think he can make it, so Beth asks if I would go so she doesn't have to go alone.

We are sitting in a semi-circle. The Rabbi is going around the room and asks people to tell why they are here. Many say it is because they feel stress because of the difference. The Rabbi calls on me and I say, "For twenty nine years I have been married to a Catholic man and we have decided in our marriage to acknowledge both Jewish and non-Jewish celebrations. For us, the dilemma isn't a dilemma and I am here to support my Catholic daughter who is dating a Jewish man."

Steve has just walked in and sits next to the Rabbi. It is the only chair available. The Rabbi turns to Steve and says softly so no one else could hear, "You know she (meaning Beth) is considered Jewish by Jewish law because her mother is Jewish." We are sitting close enough that I can hear the Rabbi. What the Rabbi and all Jewish people forget is that she was baptized Catholic and so by Catholic law she is Catholic. It is important to remember my children share their Jewish heritage and their Catholic heritage. Not one more than the other. If you look past some of the rules and fear, we all teach the same thing: Love and Trust. I don't say that out loud.

We have split up into small groups for discussion. Our group topic is on the ornaments. Tree, Nativity Scene, Lights, etc. Some of the people at our table have really good questions. I share, "For me, part of the dilemma is the control of one person in the relationship wanting very much for the other to accept their way as the only way." Ed and I choose out of respect for each other's beliefs to honor each other." Although I light the Menorah in the kitchen alone, Ed has no problem with it being there but doesn't join me. Sometimes I want him to light the candle with me but it isn't that important so I let it go. The rituals are more important than the religious part of it for me.

Well! The rabbi has just turned to me and very deliberately says, "YES, but that was your choice." He then turns to the rest of the group and says, "Psychologists today say that there must be a choice for one or the other since children cannot make the distinction between the two things." His words and the tone of his voice are reconfirming for me why I don't go to the synagogue to express how I feel about spirituality. From the tone of his voice and the look in his eye he intimidates me into being quiet. He has not spoken to anyone else like that. It is very aggressive and mean. I don't feel that it's appropriate for me to say much more even though I really want to nail the guy, because I am there for Beth and Steve, not me, and I don't want to embarrass them. I get madder and madder as the evening progresses. After the rabbi makes his little comment to me, he never looks me straight in the eye again. I know this is a synagogue and that the people are Jewish and their point of view is prominent. However, I feel like the Christians have to defend themselves. And although I am Jewish, I feel the same.

There is a young couple that has been married a very short time. He is Jewish, she is not. She has two children by a previous marriage and he has agreed to have Christmas in the home. He is very honest and says, "We went this morning to get a tree and I had this little pain in my stomach when we set it up." He also says, but I have agreed to do this and would support my wife."

This is what I am talking about. It feels respectful, honest and loving. Indeed we do things sometimes that cause us some discomfort but it is important to support the person even if we are uncomfortable.

At this point Steve asks, "What should I do if we have decided on a Jewish home but the grandparents have both in their home?" The rabbi says, "When you go to someone else's home you respect what they do in their home." Then he proceeds to say looking right at me, "BUT, IN YOUR OWN HOME, YOU MUST MAKE A CHOICE." Again I feel criticized and put down by this man who doesn't even know me and doesn't seem to care before he passes judgment.

It feels from his earlier statement he has inferred I have harmed my children by not making a firm choice. I don't ask him about it or clarify what he meant. I just get quiet.

Steve has made another comment, "Christmas starts too early and lasts too long." The young woman finally speaks up. At this point, the non-Jewish people have not said a word. "We Christians don't like it any better than you do and we wish the stores wouldn't make it so early." I am glad she said something. I feel she has to defend herself in this group. I am sorry I don't give her support.

Beth knows exactly what I am talking about when I ask her if she understands why I got angry? She feels the same way. The Rabbi also made a point to say that this issue is a non-rational issue to discuss. He is absolutely right! That is why understanding and respect is more important than having your own way. What feels like a giving in can be a loving gesture that will make your partner feel loved and accepted. We are home having dinner. Ed says, "How'd it go?" Beth says, "OK, except Mom got pissed at the Rabbi." I know at last why my parents didn't go to the synagogue. They wanted to be able to think freely with no one telling them what to think or do.

Back to the Pilling Pain Clinic

I am still working at the Pain Clinic. It's 1991 and Dr. Pilling has decided to leave and go to North Memorial Hospital. The director is also leaving. Sarah is the new manager of the clinic.

It is Sarah's first week. She has come up to my desk everyday saying, "I have to have this by 3:00." I bristle. I say to Mark, "Is she talkable?" He says, "Absolutely." I am feeling afraid because confronting someone on how I feel is still hard, but I'm going to do this anyway. I'm in her office and say, "We need to talk things out. When you tell me I have to, I won't." She says, "If you won't, I'll tell you you have to." We start laughing hysterically and I know a wonderful relationship has started. It is the first time I'm not afraid of "THE BOSS".

We are all working hard and have a mutual respect for each other. We eat lunch together everyday and Mark is the only guy. It's the middle of the month and he walks in and laughing says,"Oh boy, are we cycling together again?" We have all started having our period together and emotions run high. We work very hard but also have fun. It is the first time on a job that I have this kind of relationship with the people I work with. I am an important part of the clinic and know it.

Sarah has hired a new person. Bobbie is a phycologist. I say to one of the other gals, "I'm not too sure about this Bobbie. Will she fit in?" It turns out she is just what we need.

One of the wonderful things about the pain clinic is that we all help each other without any need for payback of any kind. If Terese needs someone to do relaxation someone does it. If Mark needs someone to do something, we do it. If I need someone to watch the desk, they do it. It is a wonderful place to be. I have never worked in a better place. These people are so committed to the patients and to each other. The cooperation is something I have not felt before.

Mind Body Connection

Sarah has just come back from a conference in St. Could and brought back two people to speak to the Pain Clinic staff who will change the course of my life. Joan and Myrin Borysenko. They are experts in something I have never heard of: Mind Body Connections.

Bobbie and I have become very good friends and when we hear Joan talk it is like a whole new world opening up to me. A few weeks later, Bobbie says, "Wouldn't it be neat to have a women's weekend with Joan?" We contacted Joan and asked if she would be willing to do a retreat on Spirituality here in Minneapolis. She says, yes. We wanted it to be intimate with no more than fifty or so women.

I'm at the first retreat. Joan is talking about angels. She is Jewish but believes in every kind of religion. Mix them up she says. "We can learn for each one of them." Angels become what I believe in. I wear angel pins, I read angel reading, I have angel cards that I read every day. It feels comfortable and right.

Politics, religion, and spirituality are all blending together to help me learn who I am and what I want. I still want nothing to do with politics or formal religion but I am Jewish and figuring out what that means. What Joan has taught me is that I can believe anything I want to. It is all right. I start accepting myself.

It's the second year and we are at our next retreat. A few of us talk and we want to learn and keep this information flowing. We decide to start a spirituality group. We meet once a month, have dinner at each other's homes and work on what spirituality means to us. Ed calls us the WOO-WOO Group. He thinks we are all nuts. He doesn't understand what we are doing and doesn't want any part of it. We don't talk about it much. I feel his disapproval sometimes and finally realized I don't have to share everything with Ed. If I don't tell him what I am doing, he can't disapprove. I believe something different; it's OK. We don't have to agree on everything. I know what I am doing is good for me no matter what anyone thinks about it. No one in my family really understands what I am doing which does make me sad but the bottom line is it doesn't matter. I'm not going to stop. I realize I have been in Al-anon for a long time and still feel stuck. I want something new, something different to grasp onto. I want to change how I feel but still not sure I know how. I have been telling the same stories for all these years. In Al-Anon we tell our story of the drinking years. We all have different stories but all the feelings are the same and I am bored with hearing myself talk. I don't want to talk about the bad times. I want to move forward instead and the old stories bring up the bad stuff. I have been in Al-anon for eighteen years and it's time to let go of the old stories about the drinking years. When I started Al-anon, it was exciting and I learned so many new things. I need that again. Will the women's group give me that?

In 1992, our little group decides to write our spiritual autobiographies. How do I feel about my religion? What does it mean to me? When I asked myself these questions before I wrote the "Why Be Jewish" piece, my understanding was not as clear as it is now so this feels like it goes deeper.

It is Yom Kipper. I am at a weekend retreat at the James Hill House in St. Paul. It's called Quiet Interlude. I have been coming to this retreat for several years. We study the fifth step of Al-anon. The fifth step is "admitting to GOD, to ourselves, and to another human being, the exact nature of our wrongs." We study several topics including shame, guilt and honesty and then talk with one of the leaders of the retreat about who we have hurt and ask forgiveness so we can let go of it. It is a very healing weekend retreat and it always seemed to be on Yom Kippur. Was that a coincidence? I don't think so. I begin to connect with what the holiday is really about. It is about atonement. I begin to believe that atonement is taking responsibility for my own behavior. The women's group is teaching me to be honest, to speak my truth, to speak out. For the first time in a very long time, I begin to trust, not only who I am, but others. I feel like I have gotten a lot of help with the weekend retreat and I understand Ed's feelings about the running group. He is an introvert and it's so hard for him to make new friends. It now makes sense to me that he would want to have this separate. I am feeling much better about all of it. And since I have my own friend to run with I don't feel as lonely. We don't talk about it. I really don't feel a need to. I am just working on letting go.

A woman has just walked up to my desk at the Pain Clinic and says, "I am here to apply for the nursing job." I feel like I know her but can't place her. I say, "Do I know you?" It turns out she is one of the organizers of the Quiet Interlude. Another connection. She has started to come to the spirituality group and become a good friend. She has a lot of knowledge of Al-Anon and helps me a lot. So with the combination of Al-Anon information and our new found women's group, my life is more exciting.

It is several years later and the women in the group have changed. It seems our new members continue to be likeminded. Women who are searching for who they are and what they want out of life. Ed is the only husband that joins us at the dinner table. He sits at the end of our dining room table and looks a little confused. But even though

I know he doesn't get all this stuff, he never makes it hard on anyone. He has known these women as long as I have and likes them all even if he thinks we are weird.

Ed has a very dry sense of humor and when it comes out, it is wonderful. He has just gotten home from work. We are all sitting on the living room floor eating snacks and talking. He says, "So what strange things are we up to tonight?" and laughs. So do we.

I have really begun to understand the impact Joan has had on my life. One being angels the other is "Jew Beads". What the heck are Jew beads? Joan always talks about the fact that Jews don't have anything to pray with. She came up with the idea and has sent me a picture of how to make them. It is similar to a rosary but the beads have different meanings. The first bead is GOD. The four smaller ones are for the Arch Angels, Urial, Michael, Gabriel and Raphael and one extra to help me call in my guides. Then one larger bead and eight smaller beads connected to make a big circle. It almost looked like a necklace. I started using them for mediation.

Joan has talked about the Arch Angels and told me that they are ready to be called upon at any time. I trust her and believe her but I want to learn more. I read books about them and what they represent. Michael is the Protector and one of the most powerful angels you can call upon. I sit and meditate and ask Michael to watch over me and protect me during my day. I always feel calm, quiet and peaceful when I call upon my angels. The feeling may not stay with me all day but it is a new and positive way to start my day. Raphael is also a very powerful angel and he oversees all health concerns. It is a stretch for many people to believe that these angels can actually come to each and every person that asks but I believe. I have learned a great deal about guides as well. Everyone of us have guides. They keep an eye on us and help us everyday. Some think of this as a higher power like in Al-Anon or GOD or The Universe. It is whatever feels right to any individual person. Joan started me on this journey and I am forever grateful to her. Not only for her knowledge but now there are many new things that I want to try. Spirituality is so prevalent in my life and I want to try everything. I am feeling better and better about who I am and how I handle relationships including my relationship with Ed. As I believe in myself more, the less I try to control him. I have learned that our minds, bodies and spirit are all connected and we can use this power to help become the people we want to be. I also am learning that it was real to feel a presence like I had when my parents died. I want to learn how to use this feeling for good.

The Edmund Fitz

Ed is turning fifty and Kitty from his running group wants his group to run the Edmund Fitzgerald, a sixty-two mile relay by Duluth, MN. I am planning a 50th birthday surprise for Ed, a biking trip to Vermont. I call Kitty, whom I have never met and say, "Ed can't do the Edmund but he doesn't know it." She agrees to wait for another year. It's a year later and it is the first time the two groups are together for running. Ed thinks it will be fun. Ed's group, my running partner and I. There are eight of us doing the sixty-two miles. Bob D. had brought another couple because we needed two more people. After we meet Bob B. and Kathy, they became an interracial part of the group.

I am going to run a three mile leg. The first time I ran three miles was around Lake Harriet. It was very windy and cold. Ed was holding my hand pulling me along. At one point he said if you run the full three miles I'll get you a running suit of your choice. I got that suit. I am just as afraid this time as I was then. Now I'm with a group of people I don't know very well.

I'm out here wondering how I am going to finish this and there is the next person waiting to start. I hand off the baton and I'm done. WOW! I am back in the van and feel wonderful. I did it. Having us all together for this race has been fun. Ed seems OK with it.

The first leg is ten miles long and the most beautiful. It' a few years later and I am going to run it this year. It is dark as I start, the sun is coming up in the distance and I feel the pavement under my feet. I have the sensation of being complete. I am running ten miles. WOW! I am so proud of myself. I am surprised how well we all are getting along. I complete the first leg as I did the three miles the first time we did this with a complete feeling of joy running through my body. Ed has not wanted me to meet them so I have tried to stay in the background but we are all becoming friends.

It's May a couple years later and the running group has gone to do a long race in Grantsburg, Wisconsin. It is too long for me so I stay home. Ed just got home. It is later than usual for this race. He is heading down to the basement to get out of his running clothes. For no apparent reason I say, "So, is everyone alive and well?" He stops short looks at me and says, "NO." My heart skips a beat.

Bob B. had a heart attack on the course. He is dead. How can we process this? Could this really be happening? What will Kathy do? They have been together for eighteen years. It's the next day after a sleepless night and everyone is sitting in our living room. We try to sort this all out. Both running groups and a few friends are here. We are so overwhelmed with sadness, we are not sure what to do or what can we do for Kathy.

One of our own dead at age fifty two. How could this happen? We are all together dealing with the unthinkable. I can't stop crying. Everyone is crying. Ed and Bob had talked about doing the Edmund as a twosome calling their team "Two guy running with a full deck." because they were both fifty two years old. Ed is devastated. We all are. I have angel postcards. I send one to Kathy every day hoping this will help at least a little bit.

With Lila Gone

Lila

Lila has had a stroke. It is 1994. She can't talk and the whole right side of her body is paralyzed. We spend almost every day for the next six weeks with her. But she doesn't make it. Ed is so sad and Beth doesn't know what to do with herself. How could Grandma Lila be gone?

We have always hoped that Lila wouldn't die first. We knew it would be terrible with Ed's dad. It is. Ed's dad is a very angry man. He has never been happy with his life and seems to take it out on all his boys and Lila. His way is the only way. I remember one Sunday we were going there for dinner and we had not gone to church. When we walked in the door, he said, "How was church?" Ed said, "We didn't go." Then his father said, " Well did you go to the synagogue?" Ed said, "No." His dad looked Ed right in the eyes and said, "Then you are nothing, nothing." We picked up the kids (they were little then) and left. Those are the kind of memories we have. Ed has a lot more of course.

He argues with us every time we see him. We are at the house. Ed's dad says, "I know why you are mad at me. I haven't given Beth Lila's wedding ring yet." We try to tell him we are not mad. Ed and his dad are fighting, screaming at each other. We know Lila wanted Beth to have the ring since she is the only granddaughter but we have not said a word about it. We never would. It's crazy. We have not even thought about it. I know he is grieving but he is also an angry, angry man.

Ed is still going to AA meetings but will not talk about feelings. I am doing all this work on spirituality and wanting to talk about feelings all the time. We are on different wavelengths again. Ed is sitting in the chair in the living room watching television and doesn't talk. He comes home from work and does not talk. He is so depressed about his mom and how his dad has treated him but I don't have any idea how to help because he won't talk. I understand why he doesn't want to have long conversations after work because he is dealing with people all day long and wants some space. But this is different. He is depressed and I can see it. When will we be together? When will we understand each other? I am alone but not alone. Ed's dad remarried a year after Lila died. We thought it would make things better it didn't. He has stayed as angry as ever. This whole experience is one of the things that has changed Ed's thoughts on talking about feelings. His dad never talked feelings, only attacked and if Ed tried to talk to him it would blow up in his face. So he has stopped talking.

I am still feeling very insecure about friendships. Even though I am starting to trust my women's group. After what happened in eighth grade, I don't think I really trust anyone and haven't for a long time. My conversation with Judy helped but didn't get rid of all the insecurity I have felt most of my life. But I also know my expectations can be over the top. Am I expecting too much of Ed and not letting him grieve in his own way? I am thinking about that a lot.

Leaving the Job I Love

It's three years later and the Pain Clinic is changing and moving. Mark is leaving and we are moving to The Riverside Campus. There are two pain clinics within the Fairview system and they want them to be combined. Sarah will no longer be the boss but the director. The new boss will be the manager of the Riverside clinic.

We have gathered at the Arboretum and spend the day saying good bye to wonderful. We know the Pain Clinic will never be the same. We walk in the woods and exchange stories. I am walking along a path and see a sign that says "End of Road" We take a picture of all of us together with our middle fingers held high. We do not want this to be the end of the road but it does feel that way. We have white shirts that we each are writing messages on for each other to help us remember, as if we can forget. Bobbie gives us all green stones that I attach on the end my Jew Beads.

We have been at the Riverside campus for a year. I have decided I need to leave. The new boss doesn't feel it is necessary for me to be in the staff meetings about patients etc. I have lost my connection to the patients and the doctors. The changes are too much. Mark is no longer here and Sarah is not working with us on a day-to-day basis. Although the staff is the same, we aren't connected like before. I have been at this job for six years. I don't think I will ever find another like it. I have no problem getting another job but none that I have ever match up to the Pain Clinic.

Phyllis

Phyllis and I are in Palm Springs. Skip is with us this year. I know she is mad at me but I don't know why. I asked her and she says, "No, I'm not mad." But I know when someone is mad at me. I can feel it. There is a difference in how she acting with me that I notice. I get quiet. Here we go again. The years before we had shared our lives and laughed and truly enjoyed each other. This year is different. Her husband Skip is along but we really liked each other so I know it isn't Skip. I know there is an issue about some socks I want. It's crazy. I keep asking them to stop so I can find them and I know I'm getting out of hand but I can't seem to stop. I also think she is not paying attention to me so she won't stop when I ask. She is mad and won't say anything. So why did she come this year? When we started to make plans to see Aunt Lottie, Phyllis said she didn't want to go. I pushed her a little, but finally said, "Fine, I'll go by myself." She changed her mind and decided come along, and to have Skip come. I think this is why she is mad but won't say so. Its not really about me. I was more then willing to go alone. She didn't have to come along. I wasn't forcing her.

Time has moved quickly. It's a couple years later. Phyllis's son is getting married. Ed and I are in the car driving to Chicago. I am surprised we are invited since I know Phyllis is still mad at me. Beth and Steve drive a few days early and we are going to meet them there. We are at the groom's dinner, I feel a little out of place and I'm not sure why. No one has introduced us to anyone. I think it's a big day for everyone and try to let it go. The wedding is very nice and everything is beautiful. We are at the reception. I walk up to Phyllis and ask, "How are you doing? Do you need any help with anything?" She says, "No." I think, she just brushed me off. We are seated at a table in the back of the room with some of her friends. I am a little surprised that we aren't with the family since we are the only family members from out of town. Beth looks at me and says, "Are we being slighted?" That's when I get it. She IS mad and she is letting me know.

Do I overreact? Probably! I am so hurt we leave the reception right away and I have been crying all night feeling like there is a hole in my heart where a friendship had been. One of the things I have looked at is do I like people more then they like me. Is that one of the problems with my friendships because I have been through this before. It's the next morning and Ed says, "Call them to say goodbye." I don't want to. I want to just leave but I make the call. Skip answers. I say,"We are leaving." I can tell he has his hand over the phone and says to Phyllis, "You have to say goodbye." All she says is, "Thanks for coming," and hangs up. I cry almost all the way home.

I have decided to write Phyllis a letter. I have learned in Al-anon and all the counseling I have done that I have to say what I saw, how I felt and what I would like to see happen. I am also learning to take responsibility for my own behavior and I know that my behavior a few years before on that particular trip had been out of line and I say so. Ed and I are out to dinner. He says, "Phyllis called and she is burning mad at your letter. I don't understand why you wrote it." He says that I should not have done that and that Phyllis was right to be mad at me. He sides with Phyllis. Now I am furious with both of them. I say to Ed, "After what happened at the wedding I had to deal with it and this was my way of doing that." 'A few days later I got a letter from Phyllis calling me every name in the book. I could hear her screaming at me through the paper. I show it to Ed and he couldn't believe how angry it is. I just say, "I knew she was angry. I just didn't know how much." Ed and I are having a pretty rough time right now. I feel he didn't believe in me. This feels like eighth grade when I was betrayed by my friends. How could he do this? I am his wife. He doesn't want me in his running group and now he is blaming me for upsetting Phyllis. How can he take her side when I have done nothing wrong. It takes awhile for me to let it go. I do but my trust in him has slipped a little.

The Wedding of Our Lives

It's 1995, Beth has always wanted a big wedding. We still don't have much money and are not sure how to pay for it all but we really want this for her. I have money left over from Aunt Lottie and say to Ed, "Let's use it". It is so worth every penny. What a beautiful occasion. It is a celebration of so much joy. It is also a healing time for Ed and I. We are both having the time of our life at this wedding. Beth and Steve look so happy. I would not let Beth ask Phyllis. I'm sorry about that now but it is what happened then.

Ed is making the father of the bride speech, He says, "Susan and Marshall (Steve's parents), Leslie and I want to thank you all for coming to the wedding ceremony of our daughter Beth and Uh, Uh .....oh yeah Steve." We are laughing so hard we can hardly breathe. More speeches are being made. One of the groomsmen is leaning back in his chair. He falls off the podium, he is fine, but again we are laughing really hard. We are creating so many wonderful memories. We are dancing and laughing and talking with all our family and friends. Ed is very proud of Beth and shows it. The look on his face for the father-daughter dance is priceless. Beth has planned the whole thing, just letting us know how much it would cost before she had a contract. We let her do this. It is her thing and she is good at it.

Theodore Joseph

Grandpa and T.J.

Theodore Joseph Hallfin is born on September 5, 1995. My birthday is September 4th. What an amazing thing to have a grandson. Ed and I are so delighted we can hardly contain ourselves. We have something to believe in together again. This little boy is so important to us. We are very connected to Beth and her family and spend a lot of time with T.J. as he is called. We babysit even if they aren't going out so we can be with him. As T.J. grows, I see Ed come alive. He shows every feeling he has ever had to this little guy and I can see how happy he is. Starting when he is about two years old, he says, "Grandpa, want to play baseball?" and to me says, "Want to go shopping?" It's pretty special.

China

Judy and Me

It's ten days after T.J. is born. I am leaving for China. Judy is in China for the Women's Conference held in Beijing. She has been traveling all over the world for the International Council of Jewish Women, so we decide to meet and do a ten-day tour of China.

I board the plane on my way to Beijing all by myself. Is this really me? On a plane all by myself going to a foreign country. How different from my trip to Germany. I am not afraid this time only excited. We spend ten of the most wonderful days I have ever had seeing the places and things in China that I have always heard about and wanted to see. I have dreamt of going to China for as long as I can remember. This trip is truly amazing. We have climbed the Great Wall, We sat on the lions at the Ming Tombs. I'm sure we weren't supposed to, but what fun. Breaking the rules. Going to the Forbidden City and the Summer Palace. We are watching the huge clock in Tiananmen Square ticking off the hours and minutes until Hong Kong goes back to China. Seeing where the students were killed in the uprising. I am struck by the beauty of the Terra Cotta figures in Schian. These figures were found in a pit surrounding an emperor's grave and put there to protect him on his journey to the other world. Emperors are known to have built huge fortress around their burial sites. No two are alike. Soldiers, officers, peasants all carved out of stone and each different. I reflect on the people in my life that are also beautiful and different. Ed and I are very different but we are so connected that I don't think anything can tear us apart. Even in the bad times, we can't seem to stay apart. My mother and father are very different. Dad was soft spoken and gentle and mom was more demanding. Some of our friends have different personalities then we do but we are still friends. Judy and I are different she is full of adventure I am more down to earth. I want to be more like her. Anita and I are more alike. We like doing the same things. She is Swedish and I am Jewish It just doesn't make any difference. Barb is much more quite than I am but we just get along so well. I think its a common respect we all have for each other that lets us look beyond the differences and just accept each other. That is what I am hoping for Ed and I.

I attribute my new found confidence to Judy. She is the only person besides Anita that I trust completely. This trip is around the same time I have had the fight with Phyllis and Judy says something to me about shopping and because shopping was the issue with Phyllis I burst into tears. Now whenever I am asked about the trip, I say, "It was great and Judy only made me cry once." We laugh and laugh about it. It is hysterical. It is the second big trip I took alone without Ed. He doesn't mind. I used the last of Aunt Lottie's money to pay for the trip.

Money

It's May 1997. Ed has come home from work and we are eating dinner. He says, "My accountant came in and says we owed $50,000 in taxes." I can't believe it. I say to Ed, "If we owe that much in taxes how come our life style has not changed?" He doesn't respond, just looks at me with a dumbfounded look on his face. He doesn't know either. We still have no money. Something just isn't right. Ed calls a friend of ours who is an accountant. Rick looks over the books and has taken over the House of Note accounting. He not only got all the money back but helped turn our life around. I still have lots of issues around money that I have never dealt with. I'm not even sure I recognize all the problems I have and why. Ed and I deal very differently with money. He comes from a poor family and I came from one that gave me whatever I wanted until the bottom fell out when I was sixteen. Yet he is the one who has taught me so much about money like how to save and how to watch what I spend.

When I look back at the money issues I have, I know I used shopping as a way to cover up my feelings. Kind of like smoking. I feel guilty every time I go shopping even if it is for something I really need, like underwear. I have my own money, so why do I feel this way? Where has the guilt come from? So many of our conversations during the drinking years were about my spending. "How could you spend that money when we don't have it?" he would yell, yet the money he spent on booze didn't count. Remembering what my grandparents had done for us around money only made me feel more guilty. During the drinking years, we asked them for a lot of money and they always gave it to us. My parents had fought and fought about money as I grew up because of the bankruptcy so I had no realistic beliefs about money at all. I carry the guilt even now, even though I know I have changed and am handling it better.

My parents had lived beyond their means and Ed is teaching me not to do that. My sister used to say, "My father never taught me how to deal with money." I said, "How could he teach you? He didn't know how himself."

Our Big House

It's January 1998. We have been talking about moving into a town-house. Ed doesn't think we can afford it. I have been out looking just in case he should change his mind.

This winter has been terrible. He has been on the roof for four hours clearing off snow and ice dams. He comes in and says, "Sell this sucker." We put the house on the market and it sells in two weeks for more than the asking price.

Ice dams form when snow and water back up under the eaves of the roof if the insulation in the house is not great. The warmth from the heat in the house melts the snow and then it freezes and builds up so that when it all begins to melt the roof more than likely will leak. It has happened to us before. He has to take a shovel and pick to break them up.

There is a set of town houses across the park from where some friends of ours live. My friend and I go for a walk around the two-mile path and I'm always saying, "I wanted to live there one day." The realtor that I am working with takes me there. There are two houses for sale. One is nice but the second is absolutely wonderful. Ed is willing to look but wants me to do all the leg work, which is fine with me. We call Ed to meet us and take him to both places. The smaller one first. As he walks into the second one, the one I like best, he looks around and says, "I could live here." We talk about buying the house.

It is probably the first time we have a real discussion about money that isn't a fight. He says, "In order for us to be able to afford the house, we would have to sell the shop in Duluth." He has opened a second House of Note in Duluth. I tell him, "I can't make that decision for you. You will have to decide what you want to do." He decides to sell the Duluth shop. We move in March. It is snowing and Barb calls and says, "Remember to tell Ed he doesn't have to go out and shovel." I say, "OH! He remembers!"

We had lived in our little house for so long it was almost paid off. We have enough money from the sale that I can get new furniture. It is so much fun shopping. Sometimes Ed goes along and we really like the same stuff but there is stuff I have picked out that he doesn't like. We are talking about it, we are making decisions together for the first time in a long time. Our new house is two or three times the size of the little house. It has five levels and lots of windows. Who ever heard of buying bigger at our age? We both love it.

Grand Canyon #1

Ed and I are just arriving in Phoenix. We have reservations to climb the Grand Canyon. Our first night we stay in a little cabin on the south rim. It has only enough room to walk around the bed. It's the next morning and we are packing our things to store in the trunk of the car while we climb down. We climb the Kaibab trail down to the Phantom Ranch, seven miles. We are getting a late start because Ed has lost his sunglasses and we are flying around trying to find him some new ones.

We are at the trail entrance, backpacks on and raring to go. The ranger says, "It's pretty late to start down are you sure you want to?" It is 7:30 in the morning. He also says, "Do you have food and water?" He explains many people walking down think they do not need food and drink so much water that it poisons their system. We have both.

We climb all day. It is so cool. Switch backs all the way down. As we walk, we could see the Colorado River way, way down below. It looks like a little sliver of water. As we get closer, it gets bigger and wider. Every once in a while we run into a mule train coming up or going down. We have to flatten ourselves up against the rocks as they pass. We both decide that is something we will never do: ride a mule. Smelly creatures.

We are heading to the Phantom Ranch to stay for two nights. It's about two miles from the end of the trail we are on. Ed's feet are killing him. His toes keep banging into the tip of his boot. I still have exercise-induced asthma. When we got to the ranch, they told us to go put our feet into the Colorado River. We sit on the bank of the river looking at each other like are you kidding. Ed says, "You go first." I say, "No! You go first." Ed holds his breath and looking at me with a scrunched up face, he puts a toe in and pulls it back really fast. "WOW! That is really cold," he says. He tries again. After he gets his whole foot in, he says, "This feels great give it a try." So one toe at a time, I submerge my feet with the same scrunched up face that Ed has. The guys at the front desk of the ranch are right: it is amazing. All the discomfort is gone.

The Phantom Ranch has separate sleeping dorms for men and women. Six bunks in each and one very small shower and toilet for each bunk house. It is great. The food is family-style and WOW! I could eat a horse. We had beef stew for dinner and I ask for the recipe. They start with twenty-two pounds of beef. I made it once after we got home using only two pounds of beef and Steve loves it. For breakfast, there are rolls, pancakes, bacon, anything you want. All the food is brought down every day by mule.

The first day we are out hiking trying to find Rainbow Falls. Ed is in the lead and we run into several people on the way that are coming back. They all say, "It's amazing and not too much farther." We walk and walk. We aren't talking much because Ed is in front and I can't hear him. We finally get there and it is spectacular. The rainbow colors of the water as it tumbles down the cliff are so beautiful. The water splashes up when it hits the river. On the way back I realize I am going to run out of water. I say to Ed, "I'm almost out of water." He says, "Oh, don't worry so much. We'll be fine." I don't believe him. I am getting scared after the ranger has told us to always have enough water and here we are with not enough. I panic more then Ed does, gloom and doom. Ed is much more relaxed than I am. His nickname in high school was "Easy Ed." As I finish my bottle of water, I see the ranch right ahead of us.

The ranger is giving a talk about the canyon and how many insects and small animals actually live here. It is 101 degrees down here. The following morning we are to climb back up to the South Rim. We are given a specific time to leave, 5:00 AM. They schedule it that way so there aren't too many people on the trail at the same time. It is dark and a little scary. I keep saying to myself, "Will we be able to find our way? Will we get lost?" As it gets light and realizing that with the switchbacks we cannot get lost, I relax and enjoy the wonderful sights. We climb most of the day. Going up is much harder on me. Ed has no problem going up. No feet problems at all. But he is watching out for me as we climb up, turning around every once in awhile saying, "How ya doing, you OK, need to rest?" or reaches out his hand to help me over a tough spot. We stop as many times as I need to to catch my breath or rest. Again we don't talk much because it is such hard work and we are concentrating so hard on just climbing. But we made it up. It's our last night we are walking around on the rim after eating dinner and I am so proud I could burst.

We are stopping in Sedona on our way back to Phoenix. What a magical place, a very spiritual place with spiritual vortexes everywhere. I have heard so much about vortexes in this new world I have entered called Spirituality that seeing them makes a lot of it come to life. The red rock is so beautiful and there are signs everywhere telling us where to find a Vortex.

Our hotel is right across the street from a Vortex and an outlet mall. I say, "I'm heading out to do my woo-woo stuff." He just laughs and says, "Sure enough, how long will you be gone?" "I don't know how long this will take," I say. I climb up on a rock and just meditate and think about things. Life in general. How this trip has felt so good. I feel so connected to Ed and being together has been wonderful. I'm not sure how much I feel of the Vortex itself but it is so calm and peaceful and the red rock is so beautiful that I am totally calm and happy. I have my Jew Beads with me and as I pray I feel secure and peaceful. Knowing Ed is waiting for me, I leave before I am totally ready. We have such a good time together walking and laughing that even when I want to do my WOO-WOO stuff it doesn't bother Ed. It doesn't feel like he is mad at me all the time like it does at home.

Ed goes kicking and screaming on every trip but once we get there he loves every one of them. He is relaxed on trips and laughs a lot. I'not sure when he started to call me "BIG LES". It may have been on this trip. I can see his face soften as he asks "So, what do you want to do today?" or, looking down on the city from The Cathedral on the Hill, he says, "This is amazing. So beautiful." His shoulders are down from his neck. No pressure, no worries. I know we both feel full of life. I feel I can do anything. I have the confidence and the power to do it all.

1998

Here we are home again and thing get quiet. I have the feeling that Ed is mad at me all the time. I do know I take every quiet minute on, I get paranoid that I must be doing something wrong for him to be so quiet and sad. I have not learned that it's not all about me yet. Things with Ed's dad are still bad and I can tell that it is taking its toll on him. I think he still misses his mother terribly but he doesn't talk about it. It's now been a year of no talking, no communication between Ed and I. I need to leave. But where will I go? My aunt and uncle have been in a nursing home for a while, so I call my cousin and ask if I can stay at their apartment for a little while. As I come down the stairs with my suitcase and say to Ed, "I'm leaving," he doesn't even look up from the TV. He just sits there. I'm sure we are done that we aren't going to get back together. We won't be able to make this work. All the old fears are rushing back.

Ed and I have not talked much. I think both of us are sure we are done. Ed called this morning. He says, "Dan died." Dan is Ed's cousin and we had spent some time with him and his wife Connie before she died and became friends with them. Connie had passed away from Lupus about six weeks after my mom. Dan had re-married and we hadn't seen him much. He says, "Dan had a heart attack and died on his kitchen floor." I am stunned and sad I just take a deep breath and say, "What?" He was fifty years old and a coach and teacher in

Belle Plaine and in good physical shape we thought. I say, "I'm going to the funeral whether you want me to or not." He says, "I want
you to go with." Beth comes with us to the wake so there isn't much
conversation. Another person that Ed really liked and respected has
died at a young age. I don't know how he will deal with this. I am
worried. I know Ed wouldn't do anything to himself but he is so depressed anyway. What will this do? We are driving to Belle Plaine for
the funeral, it is just Ed and I. We aren't talking but when we get there
and Ed sees his aunt and uncle, I see Ed feel for the first time in a
very long time. I can tell he was holding back the tears, I could see it
on his face. On the way home he cries. He talks about Dan and how
much he cared for him. He also talks about us, telling me he thought
it was over but didn't want it to be and wasn't sure what to do about
it. That he loves me and cares about me but is lost. He doesn't know
how to show what he feels. It seemed things would turn around for
us. In hind sight, we both sometimes feel that Dan had to die to bring
Ed back.

I have been home for a few weeks. It is close to Thanksgiving I
couldn't stand the thought of being away at Thanksgiving so I came
home. It is our favorite holiday. I cook the whole meal myself and
love every minute of it. I don't let anyone bring anything. I am home
too soon.

We are okay for awhile but I think the terrible things that have
happened with his father after his mother died has caught up to Ed.
Also he and Bob had become good friends, then Bob died, now Dan.
Ed has had a lot of losses. He realizes he needs help. He sees a counselor for a little while. He tells me the counselor tells him he needs to
be more present in our marriage but I don't think he knows how. I'm
not saying this is all Ed's fault. I have plenty of issues of my own that
affect our marriage. My money issues rear their ugly head and then

my low self-esteem affects everything. I feel unloved and don't like myself very much, so how can Ed like me? Ed has stopped going to AA meetings and doesn't have anyone he talks to about what is going on. I am talking to everyone. What is wrong? Why can't we just get along? I am back to complaining and bitching about Ed which only make matters worse. I want to get my voice back but I'm not sure how to do that.

When Ed gets uncomfortable with Ed, he lashes out. It is subtle but it is angry and mean and he doesn't want to acknowledge that he does that. Especially to me.

It is time for me to test my voice and I try. If he says something nasty or won't respond when I talk, I say to him, "You can't talk to me that way any longer." Speaking up, standing up for myself; I feel no one else is. He doesn't like it much. He responds by just walking away or giving me the look I begin to call the "DUMB SHIT" look. He looks at me with such disdain that I immediately get sullen, quiet and crabby. He shuts me up good. I think it is his way of controlling the situation if it is uncomfortable for him. I say, "There is that look again," and he says, "What look? I don't know what you are talking about."

What am I learning? Why is the fear still here? I don't want to be alone, I don't want things to stay the same, but I don't want them to change either. I just want us to be happy and love each other. How can I make that happen? I have to realize that I can't have it both ways. It has to be both of us or not at all.

Healing

I have tried so many different types of healing, looking for whatever information I can find to help me understand who I am and what I want. In 1999, I took a yearlong class on spiritual development. It empowered me to go farther and farther in the spirit world to learn.

In 2001, Mary, one of the members in the group, has gone to a healer. I still have exercise-induced asthma, so I decide to go see her. I am lying on a massage table and the healer has her hands just above my body and I can feel the heat coming off my body into her hands. As she does this, the healing is taking place. After two sessions, I am off all my medication. I am sold!

Bobbie and I are taking classes to learn how to do this. There are three levels and we decide to go for it. We have set up a massage table in the dining room of my house and see several people. We learn when we are doing a healing that it is not us, it is the higher power we have learned to believe in that does the work. I call this energy "The Universe". It is just channeled through us. I understand this is what the healer has done with me. I learn that I can do this. I have the power and energy inside myself to be a healer, whether I use it as a business or just to help myself and some friends. Bobbie and I try to start our own business. We have clients for almost three months, but we don't advertise or publicize it, so it fizzles out which is okay. I don't want to make any money at this. I just want to use it for good.

I have done a lot of reading and studying on the "Laws of Attraction". I have read all the books by Jerry and Ester Hicks. They are so enlightening. If you have any questions about how to get what you want. Read all their books. I did.

I also have done some work on color. Certain colors effect people in many different ways. For almost a year, I call Jamie once a month. In this hour session I learn about color and receive a healing in the process. I am learning a lot.

I am trying so many different kinds of healing. Ed really thinks I am nuts. He says, "What now?" and laughs. He doesn't like that I am spending the money, but doesn't complain about it too much. Once in awhile he will ask why I am doing this. I say, "It is to save my life." I know that everything I am trying is making me a better person. I also feel much better physically.

Gregory

Greg is coming home for a visit. He had gone to California to graduate school. He got a masters in fine arts at the San Francisco Art Institute. It is a surprise to us because he had no interest in art all though high school; he was a sports guy.

Greg asks, "I'm going to bring my girlfriend. Is that OK?" Beth and I have been planning on having a family picture taken when Greg is home and now he is bringing this girl. How would we do this? Greg walks in the door. I give them both a big hug, Am I ever glad I did. He says, "This is Stephanie, my wife." Beth and I just look at each other and say, "Picture problem solved."

They got married in Las Vegas on their way to Minneapolis. We are all sitting at the kitchen table eating dinner. Beth, Steve, T.J. and Greg and Stephanie. Ed has been golfing and we knew he would be a little late. Ed has just walked in. Greg stands up and gives him a hug and says, "Hi Dad. I'd like you to meet Stephanie, my wife." The look on Ed's face is priceless. He looks around the table and says, "Hello, what is your name again?" We all crack up. Greg has always told me he didn't want a big wedding and would probably elope when he found the right person. Later Ed and I are talking. He says, "I'm not sure I like this. We weren't even at the wedding."

We are in Sonoma. Stephanie's parents are having a party for them. We are staying in a little motel. In Sonoma, since it is wine country, they leave a bottle of wine in each room. I ask the gentlemen at the desk for "White Zinfandel". Greg says, "Mom, holy mackerel I have to live in this town." He has since taught me how to drink good red wine.

Mexico

Three of my girlfriends have asked me to go to Mexico with them for a week. A week of sun, reading and eating. I haven't traveled with them before and I'm not sure I fit in. They have traveled together before, so I stop asking for what I need.

I know that I had to eat three meals. I am not dieting like I had for so long but I'm still watching what I eat, just not obsessing anymore. When I quit smoking, I only gained about twelve pounds but because of my dieting problems over the years I have learned to eat more responsively. I just know I have to eat more or get sick. I have become very conscious of what I eat and how my body responds. After being so close to anorexia for so many years, I have learned to eat healthy and not abuse my body. They eat very little. We brought breakfast, bagels and peanut butter, skipped lunch and shared dinners. They never know how I feel because I don't say. I decide not to go the next year.

I have decided to go again the year after but this time I start using my voice. At lunch, I just say, "Hey, I want to get lunch." They always eat with me. Speaking up, telling the truth and doing what I need to do for myself is paying off. I am definitely getting to know how to take care of myself. In Al-Anon there is always the question, "What is the difference between taking care of yourself and being selfish?" In Al-anon it is said, "You can't expect anyone to take care of you, you must take care of yourself. If you don't, you will only hurt yourself." This I know is taking care of myself. We continue to travel and I continue to speak up.

Samson Edward Austin Volker

Sam and Grandma

It's 1999. Greg and Stephanie are on their honeymoon to Hawaii. Greg has called to tell me about the trip and I say, "so, when's the baby due?" Greg is kind of hesitant and doesn't say much. He calls back about five minutes later saying, "How did you know?" "Know what?" "That we are pregnant." Our second grandchild is on the way, due in January 2000, the New Millennium.

Their friends are going to give a baby shower in California. Beth and I really wanted to go as a surprise. I call Greg and Stephanie and say, "As much as I want to come, it just isn't possible." A few days later, Ed says, "You should go as a surprise for them," and books a first class ticket for us going out to Sonoma and coach on the way back. This is so much fun, being served good food on a plane no less. We ask for anything we want and the seats are huge. All this leg room. I have never flown first class before.

Stephanie's best friend is in on the surprise. We fly in without them knowing we are there. We stay at this great bed and breakfast called Ramekins, close to the downtown square of Sonoma. The beds are high off the floor and we can hardly climb in. The room feels quaint and cozy. They have six rooms all above the cooking school. A continental breakfast is included made by the students that are taking classes there. The scones are to die for.

Beth and I have to be very careful because Sonoma is a very small town and we could be seen very easily. We are at restaurant outside. We keep looking over our shoulders every few minutes to make sure Greg isn't coming towards us. We are in a cab the next day to where the shower is. Beth jumps out of the cab before it is even stopped completely. She is running up to Greg yelling at him and gives him the biggest hug. He is stunned. It takes him a minute to re-alize who it is. They are totally surprised and the weekend has been wonderful. On January 8, 2000 we have another grandson, Samson Edward Austin Volker.

Both Ed and I feel terrible. How will we get to know this little boy? He is so far away. The first few years when they either came home or we go to see them, Sam doesn't remember us. Greg says, "I finally put a picture of you on the fridge so Sam can get familiar." He is a sweet, sweet boy and when we see him it is wonderful for us. It's just not enough.

Semi-Retirement

I have left Fairview and then back to a few other jobs staying at them for about a year each. I just can't find a place that feels right or feels like the pain clinic. I want to re-create something that can't be re-created. I have learned that I have no idea how to deal with politics in the office. I am just being myself and even though I left those jobs on my own, I never have understood why they didn't work out.

I am working for a small non-profit company. It's 2000 and one of the women turns on me and makes it so difficult to be there that I give my notice. I am working on a project and tell my boss, "I will stay for thirty days". It is the Sunday after I have given my notice and I'm checking my bank account on the computer. There is large amount in my checking account. I can't figure out where it came from. Maybe the bank made a mistake. It's Monday. I'm at work and my boss calls me into her office and says, "You don't have to stay the month." They had processed my severance pay and deposited it in my account but didn't want to let me go on a Friday so waited until Monday morning to tell me. It's Tuesday morning and Ed and I are sitting at the kitchen table and I take the biggest deep breath and realize I haven't done that in a year and say to Ed, "I don't think I can look for another job." He says, "Well, let's try it with you not working for awhile. The shop is doing well, so let's see how it works." After not working for a couple months and just sitting and watching television, it is my turn to be depressed. Trying to figure out what has happened to all the jobs and why they have not worked out.

Sarah, my boss from Pain Clinic calls and says, "Are you interested in a part time job?" Sarah is renting an office from Susan and Susan is looking for part-time help. Susan does Leadership Kinesiology. She uses muscle testing as a tool for team building that she has developed herself. Muscle testing is a very quick, easy way to get clear honest answers to questions being asked. You hold your arm out straight and when asked a question and pressure is put on your arm, if it goes down fast you need work in that area; if it holds tight you are strong in that area. It is right up my alley. I am her administrative assistant. I begin to believe that all the problems I have had with the last several jobs weren't necessarily all my fault. Susan and I get along great.

Before I start working for Susan I realize I have no money. I ask Ed, "What do you think we can do about the money situation? I just don't have any." Ed says, "Write up what you need and let's talk about it." When we talk, we decide Ed will give me a certain amount of money every month. I will do all the grocery shopping and pay a couple small bills and take care of my own needs as I had been doing when I worked full time. This doesn't include any healing that I want to do or classes that I want to take. I will get extra for that. I hate having to ask Ed for money. Yet if I'm honest and open, he always pays for what I want. So, before I start working for Susan, Judy and I decide to go to Israel. We love traveling together.

Israel

Israel feels like coming home for me. There is a feeling in the pit of my stomach that has never been there before. I'm not sure what it is. We see so much of the Christian and Jewish faiths together. Abraham in one painting on one wall and Jesus on another in the very same church. How could we have gotten so far apart? How could we be fighting about something that will never be settled?

Everyone has their own beliefs and not you or I or anyone is going to convince the other they are wrong. Here is a country that has all faiths intertwined together in so much history. How could they fight each other? There is an escalation of the ongoing conflict that had started right before we left. We almost didn't go but decided it would be OK. Judy asks a cab driver what he thinks of the situation. He is Palestinian. He says, "I work here. I have Jewish friends. This is not a conflict for us. The extremists are the ones with the problem." It helps me realize the people who had accused my family of being Communist were extremists.

I want to go to Petra, Jordan and our tour group is offering an extra day trip. Judy has been there and doesn't want to go. I am told to not let anyone know I am Jewish. It could mean a more complex check at the border. It is a little frightening and nervous, but it goes fine. The joy is bigger than the fear. I go to see the Great Temple at Petra carved out of a sheer wall. It is in the movie, "Raiders of the

Lost Ark." To get there, we have to hike on a narrow path about half a mile through giant walls of rock that are all different shades of tan and brown; it is absolutely fabulous. I think I am noticing the beauty with different eyes. I am joyous and happy and alive. To get back, we ride horses and that scared me. I have no trouble getting back into Israel.

T.J. is being raised Jewish, isn't that something, and I ask Steve if he wants me to bring back a Yamaka and prayer shawl for his Bar Mitzvah when he is thirteen. I have a great time picking one out and buy it in Jerusalem. We are swimming in the Dead Sea and putting mud all over us; it's supposed to be good for your skin. The ten days we spend in Israel are great and Judy doesn't even make me cry once.

My Marathon

Ed has an idea. He says, "Why don't we run the Twin Cities Marathon together? It will be a good bonding experience." I have never had a desire to run a marathon. Twenty six miles... YIKES! Yet how can I refuse such an offer? He says, "I will train with you and run the race with you. You can pick the pace." He also asks Bob D. to join us. We train and ran together almost every day. I begin to believe I can do this. We are on our first twenty-two mile training run. We go from Lake Harriet over to Lake of the Isles, through the Sculpture Garden, down Nicollet Avenue downtown, to Washington Avenue, to the river, down River Road where part of the race will be, to Minnehaha Falls, back through the parkway to Lake Harriet and home. I am getting madder and madder. They are about ten paces in front of me. I can't hear a word they say and it's like I'm not even there. We get to the parking lot at Harriet. I start to yell. "What the hell? You said you would run my pace, be with me the whole time. This is the first long run and you left me behind." I am furious. Bob D. is a very soft spoken guy who never says a bad word about anyone. He looks stunned. So does Ed. They hadn't even realized what they had done. I have never yelled like that before in front of Bob D. The two of them stayed by my side for every other run we did together always making sure I was with them and could hear the conversation. The day of the race is finally here and off we go. It's cool and wonderful for a long run. As we reach Summit Avenue in St. Paul, there is a slight incline. I just keep running. When we get done Ed said, "I thought you would walk up Summit." I said, "If I had stopped running at that point, I would never have started running again." What a feat. I did it. My goal was to run the marathon in under five hours. I finished in four hours, fifty nine minutes and twenty seconds. A number I will never forget. I did it.

Jan has just called and asks if she can come over. After the Edmond Fitz, we have all become friends. At four o'clock after having talked and rehashed the race a hundred times for at least three hours Ed and I say, "We are starving, either go home or come out to dinner with us." She goes home. We are at Eden Avenue Grill in Edina, a little restaurant by our house. We have ordered hamburgers, French fries, chocolate malts and onion rings. We eat every bit and are not full. I have not eaten red meat in a few years because I can't digest it, but I have no problems that day. This is new, a feeling of strength I have not ever felt before, a true believing in myself, while wondering if I ever have truly believed in myself.

Running Group Changes

Things start changing with the running group. My running partner
and I are running one morning, like we have done for the last seven
years. She says, "I have decided to run with the faster crowd." I understand. I am a very slow runner. I think she means that we will still run,
but some days she would run with the faster group. I ask her, "Will we
still run most days? You'll just run a few days with the other group?"
No, she says, "I will be running with them all the time." In the mean-
time, she and Ed's partner have become fast friends and that night Ed
tells me his partner is saying the same thing to him. All of a sudden,
Ed and I have no running partners. Ed decided to take his partner out
to dinner to talk to her about his feelings which he doesn't do very
often, and tells me he says to his partner "It feels to me like the new
people you have met at the club are recruiting you but not me." She
says to Ed, "It is all in your head." That's it for him. He talked about
his feelings and was not heard. He doesn't fool around. When he's
done, he's done and he is done!

This feels like another betrayal. Why do friends desert me? Is it
because I like them more than they like me? Did I trust too much? I
just don't know. The one good thing that came out of this is Ed and
I start running together in the morning. I am much slower but we are
enjoying it. We can walk out our front door to the running path and
run for as long as we want. Usually three to five miles a day. I have

since learned that people come into our lives for a reason. Some stay a long time like Judy, Anita and Barb and others leave like my running partner and Phyllis. This has been one of the hard lessons for me to learn. Nothing stays the same.

Grand Canyon #2

Ed and I are just landing in Phoenix to do another Grand Canyon trip. It has taken two years to get reservations at the Phantom Ranch. Barb G. and Bob D are with us along with two of Barb's friends. We are meeting a friend of Bob's and her twelve-year-old son at the airport.

Barb has remained a constant in my life. I have seen her grow from a young mother with not a lot of self-esteem to the most wonderful mother, grandmother and woman. She is so knowledgeable about who she is and what she wants. I see it every time we talk or are together. She asks so many questions; she is always learning and growing and wanting to know more. I have led her to many healing things that I have done and she always says, "I just do what Leslie tells me. She has never steered me wrong." I can tell she trusts that I will be there for her no matter what. She has the most wonderful sense of humor and makes me laugh. She can laugh at herself which is a good lesson for me to learn. I see her now as a confident woman with a wonderful life that she has had to fight for. We love to go to breakfast on Sunday morning and talk and talk and talk. We share stories and I learn as much from her as she says she does from me.

This trip has started out with the same routine as the first time. Staying in a cabin on the rim the first night and packing up our stuff to leave it in the car for the next two days. As we get to the start the ranger is again there making sure we have not only water but food. We have plenty of both. After hiking most of the day, we have reached the ranch and all we want is a shower. It turns out that is not to be. The ranch has a broken water pipe that has burst and it won't be repaired for at least two days. We are heading to that same, very cold river to wash our hair and clean up a bit. The same cold river Ed and I put our tired feet in last time we were here. We have to carry buckets of water into the toilet to wash it down after we use it. It is a fun time having others with us, to share this experience with. Ed and I are laughing a lot together. It has added a bit of excitement to the adventure, but after two days we are looking forward to heading back up and we are tired and dirty.

We are all sitting around after dinner talking and Don is complaining that his knee hurts and says, "I'm not sure I'll be able to walk back up." Barb says, "Leslie, why don't you heal him." I have not done a lot of the Three Heart Balancing healing work with people that aren't in my close knit group so I am a little apprehensive about it. But Don says, "Go ahead. I'll try anything once." As we sit here talking and going over the hike down and our wonderful dinner and no hot water, I put my hands around Don's knee. There is a tingling that I feel as I place my hands on the area that needs healing. When the tingling stops, I know I am done. Forty-five minutes later, Don stands up with no pain in his knee.

Many people come down the trail a little ways and think they are climbing the canyon. They have on flip flops and don't bring water. It is pretty scary to see. They have no clue what it really takes. We are coming up from the bottom, seven miles and were feisty dirty and our backpacks feel heavy. Joey and I are leading the pack, which is a surprise for everyone, since I am the oldest woman and he the youngest boy,only twelve. As we get closer to the top, there are lots people on a casual stroll. After not being able to shower for two days and on the trail so much plus our backpacks, we must look pretty scary. We pass people meandering in the middle of the trail and yell, "Out of the way! We are coming up from the bottom." They jump out of our way. It is a hoot! Barb has never done anything like this before and is very proud of herself. We all are feeling pretty good. Again, we love traveling. We have such fun when we are off on an adventure. Why couldn't we have this at home? We feel such freedom while traveling, but not at home. At home, it is hard for me to stay within myself and be strong. We both seem more stressed when we are home. By the time Ed gets home from work he is tired of being with people and doesn't want to talk. By the time I get home I want to talk about my day. When we are on a trip we are just more relaxed. No responsibility except doing what we want to do.

40th Wedding Anniversary

Ed and I are traveling again. It's February 2004. We decided to take a trip for our 40th wedding anniversary. How can we be married for forty years? Where has the time gone?

We decide on Europe. We have signed up with a tour group for Italy, France and London. Fourteen days total. The longest trip we have ever taken.

There is a little town in Italy called Cremona where Stradivarius, the well known Italian violin maker, did all his work. Ed was told there is a violin shop on every corner. Well, just about... We fly to Italy a few days early so we can go to Cremona. We land in Milan and rent a car, our first mistake. Our travel agent has told us there are no trains from Milan to Cremona. We are out of Milan okay and on to the highway. We are told that we should drive on the right side of the highway because the Italian drivers are so fast that if we are going slow they will run you over. How right they are. They are buzzing by us at tremendous speed.

All of a sudden, there is a toll booth. Ed yells, "Oh God, we have no money." We had forgotten to exchange some before we left. Panic sets in, then right in front of us is a sign that reads Visa, Mastercard etc. Saved again. We have no idea what it will cost, but who cares; we get through.

We get into Cremona after a four-hour drive that should have taken us two. Not being able to read the signs we got off the highway too soon. We have been driving around for awhile looking for our hotel. Then there it is, kiddy corner across the street from where we are but we can't get there. We are trying to find the right one-way street that will take us there. Everything is one way. OH my! At first, we didn't realize we are on a street that is only for walking. People are yelling at us and giving us very odd looks. By this time we are both so anxious that we can hardly speak. Then there it is and a parking place right in front of the hotel. We pull into that spot and never use the car again while we are there. We try every which way to return the car so we don't have to drive back to Milan, just like the train in Glacier, but we aren't able to and know in a few days we will have to drive back to Milan.We also find out from the hotel clerk that of course there is a train from Milan that puts you right into the center of town. We won't use that travel agent again.

What a time we are having; this small little town is amazing. As we walk down to the main square, there is a marathon going on. Wouldn't that be fun to run a marathon in Italy? There is a violin shop on most streets. We have stopped at several; it is so fun for Ed. He has been in contact with a cello maker from the area who is a teacher at the violin-making school. He is giving us a private tour. The school has a library of every book written on how to make a violin. He also takes us up to the workshop to meet some of the students. It is amazing. Ed is in his glory. We walk and walk, eat gelato and the best food we have ever had.

Now to drive back to Milan. We have to catch a train to Rome and meet up with the tour group. We get into Milan okay, but cannot find the car rental return. We are driving around and around, stopping to ask several people where it is, but we can't understand them and they can't understand us. One person finally points and says, "It is at the train station." We have made a wrong turn and are up on a cable car track. By this time, Ed is in a state of shock. Why did we do this? How would we ever get out of here? Then in front of us pops a sign: CAR RENTAL RETURN. Someone is watching over us. It is UNDER the train station. We drive in, get out of the car, turn our keys in and never look back.

We are on the train to Roma, sleeping most the way and now have met up with our group. For the next ten days we are simply amazed at every turn seeing Roma and Florence. We have had the best pizza ever in Florence. Ed's favorite so far is the Sistine Chapel, mine is the David although the Vatican is spectacular.

We are in Venice having dinner in St. Mark's Square. Our tour guide has scared me. He stresses and stresses that we should not go into the inner city of Venice and says, "If you get lost we will leave without you." So we stay around the square. We did go to the glass factory and take a tour, which is amazing. We are back on the bus and several people had gone into the interior of Venice and had dinner and said people where wonderful showing them how to get back to the square. I'm sorry I listened to the guide.

Then it is off to France. The Moulin Rouge, the Louvre, the Eiffel Tower. Things we had heard about all our life and here we are. We are staying at an amazing hotel in Paris, Ed wants to go out for a walk and I am so afraid of getting lost I don't want to. It's dark and we can't read any of the street signs. He is upset with me. I can't blame him.

Now it's off to Monte Carlo, Cannes to see where the Cannes Film Festival is held. Ed bought me a wonderful sweater in Nice and we ate French bread from a little outside market.

Now London but we are getting tired. Our digestive systems aren't working so great and it has been a long trip. We are supposed to meet a couple I had met in Petra, Jordan. They live on the outskirts of London. We walk over to the tube station, which is what they call the train system in London, across from our hotel. A very nice gentleman tells us exactly how to take the tube. We have to go downtown and transfer to the train to get to the place where my friends are. We walk out of there looking at each other and say, "Did you get any of that?" NOPE! Nothing is computing. We didn't understand one word the guy had said and he spoke English. I call my friends that night and say we aren't coming.

We are at dinner. As we order our food, I want to order one thing and Ed says, "What? That is so expensive." I can't believe what I am hearing. He hasn't complained about money or anything the whole trip. He even bought me a very expensive leather jacket in Florence. It is the softest leather I have ever felt. We even spent two hundred and fifty dollars to go to the Moulin Rouge in Paris. His shoulders slump and he says, "I want to go home." I agree. I go to the office of our tour group and they won't help me saying, "When you got to London, we were done. You are with another group." I'm furious. So I go and talk to the concierge at the hotel and he is wonderful and helps me get our reservation changed. We did see Big Ben, the London Bridge, the crowned Jewels and shopped a little at Harrods. But it is time to go home. We are both so tired, we can't think.

Again as I think about our trip on our flight home, I am reminded of how much we love to travel together and how well we get along on a trip.

A Lesson from the Universe

Although I have been working on myself for a very long time, I am still having problems dealing with others. I want to change them. I want them to be who I want them to be rather than who they are. I am learning a lot, but not enough. The Universe, as I now call my higher power, has another lesson for me to learn. I have been diagnosed with Breast Cancer.

Today is February 2nd, 2005. I am going in to get my regular routine mammogram at Suburban Radiology. The next day I get a call from the Southdale Breast Center saying that they would like me to have an ultrasound as there is a small spot on my left breast that doesn't look right.

As the ultrasound technician is finishing up he says, "It is nothing to worry about. I have never seen Cancer look like this" and gives me two choices. Either I can wait six months and have a re-check or have a biopsy. right away. Are you kidding? I want a biopsy tomorrow!
I couldn't imagine anyone waiting. What do people do that feel they have no choice? The little old ladies and young women that do and believe everything their doctor tells them. I knew I could make choices for myself. There are so many that can't or don't. I had no symptoms, no physical pain at all, not even a twinge.

I haven't told anyone I am having a biopsy done. Ed is in the Bahamas golfing and is coming home on Thursday, the same day as the biopsy. I had a biopsy about thirty years ago which turned out fine in my right breast, so this didn't seem like a big deal.

I am lying on the table with a hole in it for your boob. How strange. Then they put a small mammogram machine on to hold it still. From an X-ray, they find the spot and line up the needle. The hardest part is holding still for a half hour on my stomach. I have to wait a week for the results.

I have an ice pack inside my bra to help with the swelling. I am supposed to change the pack every hour for approximately six to eight hours. I want to go to a retirement party for a friend tonight so the nurse told me most restaurants have crushed ice. Just ask for a glass, go to the bathroom and put fresh ice in the pack. As it starts to melt, I ask for crushed ice and of course they don't have it. About twenty minutes later the water started running down my side. I am sitting with another friend. and finally tell her what was going on. We are trying not to laugh.

Today is February 14, 2005. Dr. Radcliff calls me about 3:30. "Happy Valentine's Day. Your biopsy is positive. "you have Breast Cancer."

I don't quite know what to do. She is going to call me back in a few minutes after scheduling the doctor appointments I will need the next day. When she calls back I am really scared. I ask her if I should call Ed at the shop and have him come home? No, too much of a shock!

Dr. Radcliff tells me to call a good friend and stay on the phone as long as I need to talk. I call Kathy; she is a nurse. We talk and cry for about forty five minutes. She is wonderful, very supportive and positive.

I am waiting for Ed to get home from work and I am going to be very strong and tell him. Then we will talk about it. Ed is coming up the stairs. The second I see him I burst into tears, the kind of crying when you can't catch your breath. As Oprah would say, "the ugly cry."

I can't tell him what is wrong. Ed is quiet. I can't see his initial reaction because I have my head on his chest. He just holds me as I catch my breath. I have Breast Cancer, I say. He doesn't say much. He is quiet yet strong and not used to having me break down like this. He just said in his quiet voice, "This is just a blip on the radar screen and we will get through it."

We are talking about how to tell Beth. She lives close so I could drive over there and tell her but not sure what the right thing to do is. I don't want to call her on the phone just like I didn't want to call Ed at the shop. Would it be too scary for her? Ed thought it would be better to tell her on the phone. He says, "She is a Volker, you know." Meaning she would have to digest it in her own time.

I call Kathy to see what she thinks and she says to go ahead with Ed's first instinct. I call Beth and it is fine. We are both matter of fact about it and that is OK!

Tuesday I spend almost all day calling friends. I call each one of the gals in my spirituality group and cry each time. It is a very hard day.

I'm not sure why I have a need to call everyone. It just felt like something I needed to do. But I think I just I wanted the support. I want everyone to tell me this will be OK.

Beth and T.J.are here for dinner. He is ten years old now. I'm not sure if he understands everything that is happening but we act as if we are all OK and he does also. Beth is so cute. Her humor has saved the day. She said, "I told Sue today." Her really good friend. Sue is very concerned and asks Beth if I am going to have a mastectomy. Beth says to her, "Puff, if she needs one with the size of her boobs, they probably won't even need an anesthetic."

I burst out laughing just as Judy calls. Judy wants to know if I was laughing or crying. I say laughing. Beth says, "OH! Mom I'm sorry."

I laugh even harder. Humor would save many a day. I was listening to Beth and there was a light side to this if I listened.

I call my sister and tell her and she is matter of fact also, but then I hear that she called my niece Sandy, crying hysterically that I was going to die.

Ed and I stop at Beth's for lunch and then off to the Oncologist.

OH! MAN! Nurse Bob is really wild wearing a royal blue top with red decorations all over it. He weighs about three hundred pounds, has his wrist in a sling, his foot in a big cast and started telling us how he has had rotator cuff surgery and it was much worse that he thought. He also tells us he has an Achilles tendon problem but couldn't get it fixed until his shoulder healed. While he is asking me my medical history, he asks if I have any hearing loss and then says, "Oh! that reminds me. I better put my hearing aid in." Ed and I look at each other and almost burst out laughing.

The Doctor walks in and all he talks to us about is the next study that is starting in a few weeks. He never asks about me personally. I don't like him any better than the nurse.

As we were coming out of the office, Ed says, "I suppose you will want to run Race for the Cure now." I laughed and said, "YUP! Maybe even do the 3 Day Walk." I realize where Beth has gotten her humor. It is from Ed. He has a very dry sense of humor and it always cracks me up.

When I call Beth, she says, "Ask Dr. Radcliff how she picked the oncologist. If she picked him because he is the best doctor in town, you get over the personality. If it is because you could get in quickly, that's not always the best choice." I ask her and it was because I could get in right away. I asked for some other names. I make an appointment with Dr. Barbara Bowers for March 2nd. I have heard of her and she has a wonderful reputation as an Oncologist.

On Wednesday, Ed and I will meet with the surgeon. Beth told me to bring a tape recorder so we would remember what is said. She has come up with lots of good questions. My surgeon, Dr. Paul Benn is wonderful. The best thing he says is, "Don't do this around your life, do your life around this." That is what I am going to do. He said it was fine to go to Mexico and to take T. J. to California. T.J. and I have been going to see Greg and Sam for a few years.

Even though this is Cancer, I feel empowered somehow. With Beth and Ed's help, I realize I can ask for what I need. There are options that have not occurred to me, not only with Cancer, but in life. I am learning every day.

On Thursday, as I am running some errands and going to Sandy's house, Beth calls me on my cell phone and says, "Where are you? I tell her I'm running errands. She says, "Shouldn't you be home resting with Cancer?" NOPE!!! I'm running errands with Cancer. What a great sense of humor. It really helps.

Beth calls me later today and says that Naomi has called and in her outspoken way said, "So, what are WE going to do?" Beth was so stunned, she said "What?" and Naomi repeated herself. Beth said "WE are not going to do anything." Beth thought it was rather strange since Naomi has never been involved in her life. Why would she call and say that?

It's Friday and Naomi and I are out to lunch. While talking to her, I tell her that if she has any questions or concerns to please call me rather than Beth. She gets very defensive and spouts out, "I was only calling to see how you were." I say, "If you have any questions please call me rather than Beth." She gets very quiet. When I get home, there is an e-mail waiting for me telling me that what I said to her was inappropriate. I don't respond I just can't put the energy in to my sister right now. I call a friend and tell her what is going on. She suggests I write a letter to Naomi and say all the things I need to say and then burn it. I think this is a great idea. I want to do this before surgery on Friday, February 25th, so I can go into surgery with no stress other than my own. My friend says, "If you can burn the letter with compassion instead of rage it will be much more helpful." We come up with what I will say to Naomi if she calls and isn't helpful. I am doing a lot of work on the compassion part and adding compassion with boundaries. I burn the letter, then sage'd the house. Using sage to clear the house is an old Indian tradition of getting rid of stale old energy, I light a sage sick that I have bought at an Indian market using a match, it does not fire up it just starts to smoke and walk around the house slowly waving the stick in each room so the smoke gets into every space, after I do this I am much more relaxed about the whole thing. This Cancer is not about her stuff. It is about my stuff and not letting her get all the attention when it's about me. This is her pattern. I knew that if I didn't start to forgive her in some way and find some compassion in my heart it would only hurt me. She doesn't know what I am carrying around; only I do. I also know I have to start setting boundaries with her, so I don't feel so angry at her all the time. It is the only way I can start to heal.

I have also looked at my little Gremlin, I think of Gremlin's as that little voice in my head that talks and talks and talks all the negative things I think about that says no matter how much attention I get it's never enough. I have so many people that care and that have sent good thoughts and prayers. I don't need anymore. This is really old stuff and I'm looking at it very closely.

Friday the 25th is here. I have to be at the hospital at 6:30 am. Beth is with me. Ed waited until I was done showering etc and then will came as soon as he was ready.

They are taking me to the Breast Center to have the procedure for the Sentinal Lymph Node Biopsy. This is where a wire localization and dyes are put in so the surgeon can locate the main lymph node to take out and have biopsied. It takes about a half hour. It is painful to have the dye put in. They give me a shot right in the nipple. OUCH! They give me some Novocain but say it usually doesn't work, but give it to me anyway.

I am back at the hospital around 8:30 and I have to sit and wait until 10:30 am when surgery is scheduled. Ed, Beth and I are watching TV and talking and kidding around. It's like an out of body experience.

This feels like it is happening to someone else and that it is no big deal. Because everything is going so smoothly, I don't get to be a survivor. I don't qualify…WOW!

I am realizing the feelings of not being good enough are tied to all the low self-esteem issues I have carried throughout my life and it is time for me to move on. To move on, I must accept myself for who I am. Warts and all. Yet what does that mean? How do I move on from so many things I carry with me and have been for years? Where do I start to know that I am worth all good things? HOW DO I ASK FOR WHAT I NEED?

Beth brings me a little pink Breast Cancer beanie baby bear named "Cure." A pink little bear how cute, I just love it. Ed is here for the whole thing and is very supportive.

I think, here I am having a lump removed from my breast and a lymph node biopsy and I don't allow myself to think it's a big deal… It is a BIG DEAL….. and it's okay for me to say that "IT IS A BIG DEAL." And I will survive this. I hope I can hold onto this feeling.

At 10:40 am the anesthesiologist comes to get me; I'm walking into the Operating room and climbing onto the table. The nurse comments on my tan. I've been going to the tanning booth before the Mexico trip so I don't burn when we get there. She asks if I had been somewhere and I say, "Nope. I'm going next Saturday to Mexico."

She says, "really nice." She then says, in about ten seconds the anesthetic will hit your forehead. That's all I remember until I wake up in the recovery room.

Beth said later, "Mom, you looked just like the gal on "Saturday Night Live" that does the skit of a little girl in a huge rocker. So tiny in the big rocking chair with your jeans and loafers on. It was so cute." I don't even remember getting dressed.

I had surgery at 10:40 and am home by 2:00 pm. Amazing! Friday is a blur. I take one Vicodin at 5:00 pm and one at 3:30 am, and then I don't need anymore.

The flowers start coming in. A gorgeous bouquet from the House of Note staff and amazing flowers from Anita and Bob. They are just spectacular. There is a plant that looks like an orchid from Reva and Judy. Friends stop over and bring me yellow tulips and a good bottle of wine.

My cousin gave me some relaxation tapes for surgery to listen to and sent one of those spring plants that bloom inside now. It smells wonderful. People are so wonderful.

Beth, Steve and T.J. bring dinner over on Friday night and my boss made chicken soup and matzo balls. It tastes great.

Beth insisted that I do nothing. It is hard for me to do nothing even though I have just had surgery. She brought dinner, cleaned up and is just all around wonderful. She is so kind and she is always thoughtful.

On Saturday morning, Naomi calls to see how I am. Just as she called, Ed was bringing in another bunch of flowers and we are laughing because he says, "What the heck? Did someone die around here?" Naomi asks me what's so funny and I tell her. Her only comment is, "Well! I didn't send flowers. I didn't send a candy bouquet. I didn't even send a card." I just shake my head and say I know...Now what would one say to that when your only sister says something like that after you have had surgery for Breast Cancer....I have no response.

By Saturday afternoon, I am feeling better but still pretty tired. On Sunday, I take a shower and take all the bandages off. Today is Monday and I feel really good. A little sore but much better. I am meeting a friend for lunch so I can get out.

Naomi calls on Sunday and wants to bring lunch over Monday and I just don't know how to say no. I just don't want to be around her. The cleaning lady is coming and we are having the computer fixed so I just tell her it probably wouldn't work because of all that going on and she says, "I'll call you in the morning just to check." When she calls I tell her it won't work. We would have to spend the whole time in the little bedroom with the door closed. She says, "OH! It won't work for me either now."

My mind races as I try figure out what it is I want from Naomi. Why do I still want the connection with her so badly? There are so many stories out there about loving sister relationships. Is that what I have been looking for all these years? I had all these expectations. Everyone else was gone. I just couldn't let go. I realized that there was a lesson in there for me to learn. Sometimes I wonder what I would have said if Naomi ever asked what I wanted?

When we were growing up, I would have wanted you to not be so angry all the time. To have wanted to spend time with me. To protect me if someone was treating me badly, to stick up for me. If when I was hurting, you noticed and comforted me and told me things would be alright even if it wasn't true. To understand that I was never in competition with you, that I only wanted a big sister to love me. I would ask you to see me as the person I am, not the person you want me to be. As I would have done with you. I would have wanted to feel comfortable climbing into bed with you if I was scared at night, which

I was a lot. I would have asked you to ask me things not demand things of me because I was younger. Answering this question begins helping me make peace.

Ed and I are at my appointment with Dr. Bowers. WOW! What a difference a doctor makes. We are so impressed. She explains everything and she is very supportive. She says, "I will be with you through all of this. If you have pain and don't have an appointment for three months, call and we will do everything we can to ease your mind. We will be together for years." I am so glad. I tell her what the doctor at the ultrasound had said about waiting six months for a biopsy. She says, "If you had waited for six months, you would have needed chemo." She is the head of the Oncology department at Fairview and added that she knew there were problems and she was taking care of them. Her husband is Dr. Olson, the Radiation Oncologist. I will see him for radiation.

She said since the surgery is all scheduled and everything seemed in order she will schedule radiation for me after I get back from Mexico.

Dr. Bowers has kept her word for seven years now. She has been there for whatever I needed. Picking the right doctor is so important.

Then, we are off to see the surgeon. He clears me for everything. I don't need to go back to him at all. He took two nodes and both were clear. I still have to do the radiation and hormone drug therapy but I will do whatever it takes to get better.

It is March 5th. Kathy, Barb and I are off to Mexico. It is just what I need. We are out in the sun, reading good books and eating good food. They let me talk and cry all I want. It is really helping. It is just what the doctor ordered.

I am reading a book called "The Elegant Gathering of White Snows." It affects me profoundly. It is about friendships and women and taking risks.

There is still a contradiction for me. I am trying to stay very positive and focus on only the positive parts of this and then it puts me back into a place of it's "no big deal" and then I get sad. I know it is also about getting attention for myself and since I never ask for it but want it, it's a contradiction. But how much is enough? Beth and Ed have been wonderful, my friends have all been supportive and there for whatever I need.

Some of the insight I have from Cancer is that life is a contradiction. It is the way I learn by seeing two sides of issues and trying to figure out which is best for me. And of course learning how to speak up for what I want or need.

I decided in Mexico that I want to get a tattoo on my ankle to always remind me that I did this well and that I'm a strong person. I want a yellow rose because that is my favorite flower and has helped me remember who I am many different times in my life. When I started Al-anon right after Ed's affair. I couldn't stop thinking about it and it was becoming an obsession. I knew the affair was over, so why was I still thinking about it. One of the gals in my Al-anon group said that one of the ways to get rid of all the old negative thoughts is to repeat and repeat a word that made me happy. I would drive down the street holding onto the steering wheel of the car so tight that my fingers were turning white and saying "roses are my favorite flower" for miles. It worked. Soon I realized I wasn't thinking about it so much. A single yellow rose on my ankle means strength to me.

I am still feeling tired and my boob aches but does not hurt anymore. Today is March 17th. I have a bone scan and will get the results on Tuesday. I went to the dentist and have an abscess that needs to be fixed before I can start radiation. I will do that when I get back from California on the 30th. I am all set up for radiation starting April 4th, Mom's birthday.

I am back from California. T.J. and I have a good time with Greg and Sam. T.J. and I always have a good time together.

I'm starting radiation today. I'm not supposed to wear any underwire bras, perfume or lotions. Radiation does not hurt. They make a form that they use every time I come. It is to make sure they always have the right spot. They put little tattoos around the spot also. They put the form on me and set the radiation machine over it. I felt a slight tingling in my breast that is kind of weird but no pain. I go the same time every day for thirty-three treatments. Five days a week, no weekends, which is standard.

I'm not sure why but trust seems to be coming up as an issue. I fell sad today. I know I am staying way too busy; my perfectionism is getting in the way. I have to start letting myself relax. I cry at TV shows but not over Breast Cancer.

I wonder what I'm holding in. I just know I have to slow down. When I get uncomfortable with myself I speed up. During this time, A couple friends and I decide to go to Chicago for the weekend to see Joanie Borysenko.

In her talk on Friday night, Joan talks about Cancer patients. I had no idea this would be the topic. She talks about how after we are diagnosed, we are in the betwixt and between. We are different than what we were but don't know who we will be yet. It feels so perfect. I feel exactly that.

I know I am changed but where that will lead me, I don't know.

I have had 25 radiation treatments. I have to take today and tomorrow off because my skin is pretty red. It feels burned. I'm tired and a little down.

My creative side has come back some, which I am glad about. I did painting on a pair of jeans like I used to do when the kids were little. I am making bracelets for the Radiation Technicians which is really fun. I haven't felt like meditating at all. I have been doing the Dance of the Four Directions on days that we run. But I'm feeling a little down and trying to let it be OK.

The one thing that has come up is the word betrayal. Does it fit? Do I feel betrayed by God! I have taken such good care of myself and my body that I question it. But I also know what is coming from this is GOOD! Again it is the betwixt and between and chaos.

I had never had a strong faith. I had never been a religious person but I knew from somewhere deep down that what was happening was all supposed to happen. I was learning I didn't know where it was coming from, but that was the faith part. I didn't need to know I just knew.

I am done with radiation. It is a very big letdown and I am crabby. You meet these wonderful people and as Bobbie says, there is instant intimacy and then you are done. I'm glad to be done but it also feels weird to be done.

I have done some research and found out sadness or depression is not uncommon after treatment is over. I got so connected to the women in the Radiation department. They felt like best friends and then it was over. No wonder I feel depressed.

I have so many feelings. Ed and I are talking. He lets me spout off; he is great. I'm not sure he fully understands but he is listening. It boils down to attention, just how much do I need. The best way to put it is "my fifteen minutes of fame" are up. Now what do I do? I'm back wearing my regular bras, perfume and using my body oil etc. If life is back to normal, whatever normal is, why don't I feel normal?

I did a fifteen minute meditation today and what came up was – it is time to let go….let go of all the old gremlins that aren't working anymore. To be at peace with myself and this Cancer, go on with my life and let go of expectations of everyone while asking myself how do I do this?

I have done mediation on and off. I know that if I quiet my mind and let the Universe talk to me, the information I get is always positive. I sit quietly in our second bedroom that I have made into my spirituality room. I have all the tools that I use to help me stay centered and balanced in my life. I use a deck of Angel Cards. Shuffle the cards and pull one to see what the message is. I then keep track of that message in a little journal. I mediate on the subject on the card and write down what comes into my mind. I look at the expectations I have of those around me. I am learning that they are mine, not anyone else's. If they don't know about them they can't do anything about them. It becomes mine to deal with.

I had to stop all medication for menopause because I have estrogen-fed Cancer. Estrogen-fed Cancer is when there is too much estrogen in the body. I had been using a cream that I had made at a compound pharmacy, which means they mix it right there. It is a prescription but not made at a drug company. It is considered a natural form of prescriptions and it had helped my hot flashes and night sweats. Because it had both progesterone and estrogen, it fed the Cancer cells and the tumor. I used this cream for about ten years. From research I have done, I have learned we all have Cancer cells in our body. They don't know exactly why it starts to grow in some people and not others.

I started Armidex, a medication that is supposed to help keep Cancer at bay, on May 31st. It caused hot flashes and night sweats almost every hour on the hour during the night. I called Dr. Bowers and she has put me on another med to counteract the Armidex. The side effects are so bad, I have decided to stop it all.

I make an appointment with Dr. Bowers for next Tuesday to tell her about my reaction. Dr. Bowers is in complete agreement that I should go off all the medications. I am very relieved. Because my Cancer was caught so early and it was a very small tumor and they got it all in surgery, she feels I don't need to take the medication for the five years that is recommended.

It's June 3, 2005. I got my Tattoo today and yes, it hurt, but it is great. I am so proud of it. It is really everything I want it to be. And the reason I did it are still very profound for me. It shows for me and me alone the courage and strength I have had through this. I have looked at many issues in my life through this. Ed loves it, so thats a wonderful side effect. He didn't believe I would do it. When someone asked me about it, he would say, "Oh ,she won't follow through with that." But I did.

Today is November 19, 2005. I am seeing a counselor because a lot of the feelings that are coming up just didn't feel good so I want to get a different voice on the issues. The first couple sessions are about the Cancer and the attention issues. I tell her it is like it's like having Cancer never happened to me as far as my family is concerned. They never ask about me. They are not concerned at all and it's like I have become invisible again like I was before Cancer.

I realized that instead of having all the thoughts roaming around in my brain I could ask if they were real. Ed and I are out for a walk one day and I say, "Why don't you ever ask about the Cancer and how I am feeling?" He say, "I never mention it because I thought it was something you wanted to forget about. It doesn't mean I don't care. I just thought it was something you would have wanted." It was a bad experience so forgetting about it was what he would want, if it had happened to him. I say, "This is something I can never forget about. It will stay with me forever. I think about it all the time and worry that it will come back." We have such different perceptions about this. I know because I am growing so much from this and feel it is a turning point in my life, I will always remember it.

I'm not sure where this is all leading to but I know that I am different and am trying to figure out how to speak up for myself.

One of the things I know for sure is that throughout the treatment and all the issues that I have had to think about that I have done Cancer not as a victim but as a survivor. I will not feel sorry for myself any longer but learn as much as I can from the journey. I am changed and for the better. I never asked "WHY," only what can I learn from this? A year later I did the 3 Day Walk, sixty miles in three days. What an amazing accomplishment. I feel so confident and strong. I get a second tattoo the week after. A beautiful butterfly on the back of my neck. The butterfly symbols freedom in Al-Anon. I feel free.

The rest of my story could not have happened if I had not had Cancer. It woke me up. It started me on the true road to healing.

Anita

Anita passed away on April 14th, 2007 at 6:20 am.

We have been friends for thirty five years. Anita, Bob and their two boys moved in two houses away from us when we lived in the little house on Virginia Avenue. She and Bob went to all the parties on the block. All through the tough times with Ed, she stood by me. She would be honest and tell me what she saw. If I would complain that Ed was not doing something I thought he should do around the house or whatever she always said, "It's your own fault. You have spoiled him rotten. He doesn't know all wives don't do what you do." We talked about everything. All through the drinking years with Ed, she stood by us. When the affair became public knowledge, she didn't like what Ed was doing but she loved me and was a great support for me. She helped me try and figure out what to do. Every time I found out about it I would talk to her and ask what I should do. She never told me what to do just listened and supported whatever I decided.

After we got in to AA and Al-Anon, we didn't see each other as much. We met so many new friends in the program that I let the relationship slide, but the connection was always there and we knew it. The relationship was like Judy and I; even if we didn't see each other much we were connected. When we did it was like we had seen each other yesterday. She felt like the sister I never had.

After twenty eight years in the little house we are the first to move away from the block into a town house. I think it surprised everyone. We thought we would all be there forever. A couple years later, they moved to Plymouth. Although the connection was still there, we again didn't see each other as much.

It's April 2006. "I have Cancer, Rectal Melanoma," she says. "My primary doctor has misdiagnosed this and keeps telling me it is my hemorrhoids." She finally insists on a rectal specialist. She tells me, " During the first examination the doctor says that not only is it a tumor but it is Cancer." I am at the hospital Anita is having surgery to remove her rectum, and a full hysterectomy. She comes out of it very well. A few days later, Bob and her boys are told that if she lasted four months she will be doing very well.

She tells me, "Well, if I have to do this, I will do it." meaning the colostomy. She shows me how it works and what it looks like. Anita tells me, "I don't want to know how long I have." No one tells her the four month scenario. She is going to have radiation and chemo. She will have chemo every three weeks at The Hubert Humphrey Cancer Center. It's her second treatment. It takes five hours and I am sitting with her. Bob brings us tuna Subway sandwiches and we talk and talk. What are we talking about? Everything. About our friendship and reaffirming to each other how much we mean to each other. I am able to tell her what a good friend she has always been to me and she is able to tell me how she feels about her illness. We don't talk about death out loud but know it is there. It also gives Bob a chance to get out a bit. He knows he could leave if I'm there.

I spend at least one day a week with her at home and talk with her every other day. We laugh, talk, cry and just hang out together. Anita has always told me that the only two people in the world she can talk to about STUFF is her sister Monica and me. What an honor it is to have her in my life no matter for how long.

For years, our favorite thing to do was go out to lunch and shop. Whenever we would go shopping she never would spend the money right away. She would have to go home and think about it. Sometimes I would just laugh and say, "You can afford it. Go ahead and get it." Those are the times she always loves what she buys. We laugh about it as I sit on the couch with her rubbing her feet. We would have lunch for two hours and then continue on with the conversation while shopping. We never run out of things to talk about. We also went for a walk together every day after work when we lived on the block together. For awhile, we still went out to lunch and shopping but she became too weak and said, "I don't need anything now."

Bob is a wonderful caregiver. He does whatever she needs even if it is changing her colostomy bag. He has taken over all the house chores and cleans the house including the bathrooms. He has even given her an enema when she needs it. His whole world is Anita.

Bob and I have talked a little bit and he tells me that as hard as it will be without her she wants him to carry on for their sons and for their two little granddaughters and he will do that. She tells me her biggest regret is that she will not see the little girls grow up and she's afraid they might not remember her. I tell her, "Mike and Mara will not let the girls forget you." She doesn't believe in all the energy stuff that I do, but I know she will be able to watch over them always.

One day at chemo she says, "I don't want my death to be painful." I respond with, "They will give you whatever you need. Don't worry about that." Bob also says to me, "She always wanted to die first." I never knew that.

She tells me she and Bob have written their wills, met with the minister, arranged with the church for the service, and prepaid burial expenses. They understand that this is not going to get better. So do I. I feel sad all the time. What will I do without her? It is the first time I am experiencing this process. When my family died, we didn't talk about death. They didn't plan; they acted as if it wasn't going to happen. Bob and Anita are honest and open about death. Even though it is hard, it is refreshing to see.

When Anita's sisters found out that she was dying, they came to see her. Monica and Katrina came together and Gudrun came next. We have spent many hours together over the years when they came to visit. Like Anita and I, they love to go out to lunch and shop. Things in the United States are so much cheaper than Sweden so they always buy a lot when they are here. They are like family to me. (After Anita died, I went to Sweden to see Monica. It was a trip that Anita and I had always talked about doing, but never did.)

It is nine months later and the doctors have said there is nothing else that can be done. Hospice is coming on Wednesday to the house to set her up. I think she knows it is close because she has really gone down hill fast. I am there as we sit on the couch. I rub her feet and legs again. She says it feels good. We laugh about our wonderful husbands and how they just don't get it in the kitchen no matter how hard they try. She has such a wonderful spirit.

Bob has called Monica and Katrina to tell them that it is close. They want to come and be here at the end. On Wednesday, hospice came and on Thursday, I spend three hours with her. She is in a hospital bed and having trouble getting her words out. She is frustrated because she knows she is talking funny. I just tell her, "You are probably dreaming when you close your eyes every few minutes and when you wake up you are talking about your dreams." She smiles and says, "Maybe you're right." Again I ask if she wants a foot rub and she says, "Yes." I am so grateful that I can be with her.

I am on my way to pick up Monica and Katrina at the airport. It's 6:10 pm on the 13th and we go straight to Anita. We know she is aware that they are here but she isn't talking anymore. She is rolled up in a ball. We know it is very close. We all stay by her bed and talk to her and tell her it is okay to leave us. Bob is telling her to let go and be at peace. We are all sobbing.

Before I leave, I am able to sit with her and tell her that Ed and I love her and will miss her terribly. Ed is here with me but he can't speak; he is too upset. I know she hears us talking, just like my dad heard me. It is 10:30 PM. I'm feeling it is time to let the family be with her alone. I know that I have grown up. This is the hardest thing for me to do but I do it. I go home. Where have the words come from? I don't know. But I believe in angels and a higher power and they have helped me get through this.

I don't sleep well because I know I won't see her again. Its 6:30 Saturday morning and the phone rings, Bob says, "She left us at 6:20 AM and she was very peaceful."

Kathy and Mary Lou have come to the funeral to support me. Kathy understands my heartbreak because of her loss with Bob B. The minister asks if anyone wants to say anything. She gets up and says, "I didn't know Anita well. I only met her a couple times but knew about her from Leslie and she loved her so much." I am so shocked and thankful that she has said something. At this point, Ed, Beth and I are crying so hard we can hardly breathe. Anita's son Steve gets up to pay tribute to his mom. It's amazing. Her sisters get up and sing a Swedish song. They loved to sing with her. It is a beautiful service.

I miss her every day. The sadness I feel is so real but there is no fear or regret because I know I will talk to her again.

I started seeing a woman who does channeling. The first person after my parents that came to me was Anita. I could feel her with me. She told me she understood now and that everything was okay. It reaffirmed my belief in the afterlife and spirits

Another Running Partner

There is a customer of Ed's at the shop that is a runner and she and Ed have started running together. What is it with Ed and the women in his life? He always finds women to run with. They like him. He's very charismatic. I have met her and think she is very nice. We get along fine. I seem to always accept these women in Ed's life even though I am not a part of the relationship.

As I have mentioned before when people run together, training for marathons they get pretty close. They share very personal things with each other and I notice this is happening with them. Her children play the violin so Ed also knows them. She is divorced and from what Ed tells me doesn't see her own father often. So, it seems Ed can fill a void in her life. She has invited him to go to grandparent's day at her children's school. He said yes. I don't like it and think it's a little over the top for her to even ask, but I don't say anything, because I'm making a choice to let go of some of the control I feel about Ed's choices. I ask myself: would it do any good to tell him not to go? No, I don't think so. Do I have the right to ask him that? He is a big boy and can make decisions for himself. I like this new way of thinking because the control isn't working. It is different than the old drinking thinking, where I would have thought that his thinking should be the same as mine. He doesn't think like me and it's okay. This is a new awareness for me of another way of letting go to find peace. It's work in progress.

She and Ed have been talking about her opening a book store. Ed said to me, "I have been wanting to find something else to do besides the violin shop and this sounds interesting." They start researching. Ed has involved me in the process and we have gone together and looked at several stores just to see how they are doing. It is fun to see Ed really excited about something.

Then he says, "Maybe Beth would like to do this with us." She loves books and is looking for something new. Beth and this women have never met so Ed wants them to get together to talk about the possibility of working together. The three of them are at Beth's house talking. Ed tells me when he gets home, "This women said something very personal to Beth that I told her while we were running." Beth is livid and says to Ed, "How could you tell a perfect stranger something so personal about me?" It all blows up in our faces. From that moment on Beth wants nothing to do with the book store idea and absolutely nothing to do with this women. I am in total support of Beth. She is furious with Ed. When Beth and I talk I completely understand how she feels. It is such a betrayal. And yet this women also betrayed Ed. How would he know she would say anything to Beth. This women has broken Ed's trust also.

Here I am again. There is a woman in our lives that Ed has a relationship with and it isn't me. It's Thanksgiving night. Everyone has left after a wonderful holiday. Thanksgiving is our favorite holiday. Good food, no gifts not expectations. I have had too much wine and don't realize what is bothering me until everyone leaves. I am very upset with the idea of having to deal with another women in our lives. I start screaming at Ed. He has gone to bed and I am sitting at the kitchen table. "What does she want to be: your wife or your daughter? You have a daughter and a wife. You don't need more of either." As I sit there sobbing, Ed comes down the stairs and quietly says, " Leslie, just come to bed." He knows better than to say much more. I tell him I'll be up in a minute. I sit there and cry for what seems like hours. I finally go to bed and the bed is spinning. The next morning as we are having coffee and lots of it, I say, "I need her to be out of our lives." He says, "I will stop running with her." The book store idea goes away. Why does this keep happening to us? I want to look at it but it is so scary. What if he tells me he doesn't like me and finds other women more attractive than me? Ever since the affair, I feel I have not been attractive enough or good enough, even though it's been more than twenty years. If I gain a little weight, I'm sure Ed will not like me or love me anymore. He doesn't say this. It's my obsession. I think about it all the time. Weight and money. Will they be with me for the rest of my life? I don't know.

These women that keep coming into our lives reinforces these feeling in me but I also don't talk to him about it. What if I am right? What if that little voice in my head that says, "You're not good enough," is right? I get my voice back then lose it again over and over. I still have so much fear. Although these women are out of our lives now, but I still wonder when I will be his best friend and when he will want to be with me rather than someone else.

What would I say if Ed asked me what I want from him?

I would like to not feel invisible. I would like you to remember what I tell you like you remember things for the shop. I would like you to ask me what I would like and listen to the answer. I would like you to acknowledge that I am kind and generous. That I do a lot for you because I love you and want to do it. I would like you to just notice. It would be nice when I came home from being out if you acknowledged me by saying hello and asked me how it went, no matter where I was, so that I knew you were glad to see me because you missed me. I would like you to think of me first once in a while. That does not mean buying me things but saying things like: great dinner, great idea, or I missed you when

I have been gone. I would like you to know that sometimes I really know what I am talking about. I would ask you to trust me. It would make my day brighter if you said good morning. To not always say no as your first response but to think about your answer. I would ask you to understand that I have a right to ask for what I need or want.

It Starts in December 2009

I have not seen Naomi or talked to her in four years. I get a matter of fact email from her in December of 2009 that her oldest son Jim is in the end stages of liver disease. I am sad and I have not seen Jim for many years because he lives far away. He was the first of her children and a delightful little boy. I babysat for him a lot when he was little. He was my first nephew, I was only thirteen when he was born so I spent a lot of time with him. I am glad that she has told me this sad news. She asks if I want to be kept informed about his condition. Absolutely. All this is by email so I am not sure of the emotion. I can only guess it must be terrible to lose a son. How do mothers deal with that? Because we have not seen each other for so long, I don't feel I can ask. I ask if she needs anything. She says no.

My niece Sandy, Naomi's daughter, has kept me up on the details and shares her emotions around losing a brother. She is having a hard time, so I try to imagine how Naomi feels. Naomi has sent me updates for the last few months and then by email, she let me know that Jim had passed away and wondered if I wanted information about the memorial service she was going to have to celebrate him. It's so hard to read emotion in an email. I could only imagine how horrible this is. She only communicates through email; we never talk.

The memorial service is at Naomi's house. She has invited many of Jim's old friends and family. Jim loved music and John Lennon most of all. Ed and I have just arrived. Everyone is standing around visiting and remembering. It feels like a celebration of his life. There is laughter, memory books to look at and wonderful stories. I had sent her roses and brought a contribution to the place they have chosen to donate money. I see Naomi and give her a big hug saying "I am so sorry all this has happened." She has tears in her eyes.

We are here with most of my family that I have not seen in a long time. I am worried and tense. I'm not sure I should even say hello to my nephew Shawn? We have had a disagreement and although we had been going to lunch for the last few years every few weeks, we had not seen each other in a long time. He comes up to me and gives me a hug.

Ed and I walk into the screened porch and there is one of my high school friends. I am so surprised to see her. I say, "Wow! What are you doing here?" She responds almost yelling, "Well, I am friends with Naomi, IS THAT OK WITH YOU?" Ed and I just look at each other and say, "Well, of course. We are just surprised to see you." This sets me back some because the same thing had happened with another friend. She had become friends with Naomi and we don't see each other anymore.

This has been a very good celebration of Jim's life and I am glad Ed and I came. We are leaving and saying goodbye to everyone and my friend is leaving at the same time. We are standing on the front walk saying goodbye and I casually say, "WOW! Well I made it through that."

The next day the e-mails start. When I see Naomi's name on an email my heart starts pounding. What have I done now? Although I have dealt with this over and over again, my heart still starts to pound and my stomach hurts.

I usually ask Ed what I should do. He says, "What do you want to happen?" "For this to go away," I say." "Then you know what to do." He means delete it. The email is to both Sandy and I saying, "A friend of mine who used to be a friend of Leslie's has told me what she said yesterday at the memorial, that she was glad she made it through that." She took out of context what I said. I meant I was anxious and tense because I had not seen anyone in my family except Sandy for four years. It went well and I was relieved. This confusion is what emails do. They misconstrue what a person means or is saying because there is no emotion in words alone.

I call Sandy and leave a message on her phone saying, "Have you checked your email? There is one from your mother to both of us. I think I will ignore it." Sandy calls later and says, "Well I'm not going to ignore it." She sends a very loving email to Naomi, a blind copy to me, explaining that she feels the same way I do and that the nasty emails have to stop. They don't. Although this is familiar, it still surprises me. She has just lost her son, wasn't that enough trauma for now? I guess not. It goes on for days. The terrible emails telling not only Sandy, but her whole family. Then she sent them my children, saying how terrible I am. I don't answer them. Shawn emails me a long email about my relationship with his mother and thinks we should go to counseling. I just don't respond; it's too much. Naomi then asks if I want to go to counseling. I say, "I don't think counseling is right for me at this time. Why don't we just start trying to accept each other for who we are and go on from there?" We do try.

We are at a family gathering. Naomi has come over to sit with Ed and I. We are having a nice conversation. I don't share personal things with her but she also doesn't ask. We are just talking about the party, just visiting. She calls me a few days later to see if I can go to a play with her. "I'm sorry I can't I already have tickets and am going with a friend." I hear the next day she has told a relative, "Well, I tried to have a relationship with Leslie, but I'm done." We haven't talked again now for a very long time.

Previously I had been talking to Susan (my boss) about my relationship with my sister. She said I have an illusion about what I expect a sister to be. She is right.

My illusion is that she should always look after me, always protect me and be kind and loving to me. Susan said, "You must grieve this illusion because it just isn't real." I agree.

She says, "Go to a cemetery and really grieve." I know right where to go. Mom, Dad and my grandparents are all buried next to each other. I haven't gone there a lot because I feel they are always with me. If I need them, they will be there and I can talk to them whenever I want.

I'm walking in the row of headstones. It has taken me a little while to find them. There are so many new ones added since I have been here. I put my hand on the top of my mother and father's stones and look up into the sky and yell, "You had a tough time with her and now you left her with me! What am I supposed to do?" They say that they are sorry, but I am the strong one and can do what has to be done. I sit down on the ground in front of their stones I can feel their presence. My body gets tingly and I start to breathe deeper. The air around where I am sitting is warmer and I just know they are with me. "Leslie, go on with your life and let go of the sister you want. Accept the sister you have. She is there to teach you many things." "She is there to teach you compassion, forgiveness and understanding but also how to set boundaries and how to speak your truth. To gain your voice." I ask, "How did you handle the anger?" "We didn't handle it very well; we didn't know how." I get up to leave and I rub my hand over my grandmother's stone. She is right next to my dad and I say, out of the blue not knowing why, "Why did you tell us everything was so wonderful when it wasn't?" Immediately she says, "Because after Russia, everything was wonderful." I stop short, not expecting this conversation and look up to the sky. I felt my chest tighten and know what she is saying to me is right. It is like a ton of bricks hitting me. I have never experienced anything like she had. Escaping from Russia with a small child. Having to escape a terrible life of hardship and poverty and prejudice. She is right! I can feel it in my heart. I stand with my hand on her stone for a few minutes. I can feel her with me just like I felt my parents. The same warmth rushes over me. She is reminding me of what an amazing life I have. She says, "With all the anger around you, you have still kept your childlike innocence. Over and over again, you believe in people." I kept believing in Ed and somehow thought if I did enough work on myself, things would be okay. I was hoping the same for Naomi. I have never lost sight of the work I want to do on myself

"Why did you love Naomi more than you love me?" I ask my grandmother. "Because she needed it more." I don't think I ever had an understanding of anything as well as I understand her comment. I am strong. I can do what needs to be done. It feels so affirming. They did believe in me. I don't think I ever knew that.

I am on my way Bobbie. I figured I might need help making sense of what happened at the cemetery. There was a lot going on in my head about what has just happened. Previously Bobbie and I had done sessions together using Eye Movement Desensitization and Reprocessing (EMDR), which is eye movement with visualization. You also use head phones that make a sound in your ears alternating one ear at a time; it helps you relax. This process has helped with some other issues I have had over the years and I think it will help with this one. I sure hope so.

I am lying on the massage table at Bobbie's and we are doing EMDR, I am relaxed and a visualization comes to me. My wonderful little grandmother tells me that because I am so strong I don't need the attention that the others did. She says, "I didn't love you any less.

I have loved you, meaning my cousins, all the same; some just needed more attention than others."

My visualization takes me to my favorite place. A dock on a small river with a field of yellow daises in front me. My feet are dangling in the river.

My grandmother has her arms around Naomi and I am in sitting in front of them. There is a cord from Naomi to me, a thick heavy white cord. As my grandmother tells me she loves me, I am able to let the cord with my sister go. It is like a powerful spring and snaps back to my grandmother after I let go. I feel a new kind of understanding around this relationship. As I come out of the EMDR I understand so much more than I ever have and I truly believe that it is my grand- mother telling me about her truth that has helped me come to mine. It is a beginning of letting go of things that no longer serve me. Ac- cepting my relationship with my sister really is a relief. I have no fear of not having her in my life if that is what happens. It feel peaceful and calm. But I guess the emails still bother me.

I am growing up. I have a great deal of compassion for Naomi. What I have learned over the many years is to set boundaries around this relationship. If that means not seeing her or talking to her, that is the way it will have to be.

I have just finished a book called *Pigs Eat Wolves* by Craig Davis. It is an amazing little book. The book discusses what the three little pigs may represent and what the wolf may represent. The pigs are in three different stages in life; the wolf is our dark side. The first little pig is in that place in life when we leave our home and take with us what our parents taught us but we don't go beyond that. The wolf eats him. My early years were that stage.

The second pig is the same but with knowledge that things can be different but he doesn't know how to change it yet so is not able to fight off the big bad wolf. He gets eaten. This represents the years of discontent until I learned I could do something about my life and change it.

The third pig builds his house of brick. A solid foundation to live in. He also goes out and plants a garden not afraid that the wolf will eat him like he did his brothers. But is this safety a prison? Can he leave his house and not feel afraid? What are the risks? This is the part of my life I am living now. I have come up against the big bad wolf and I'm risking everything to not be afraid and become who I want to be in this life.

This has been one of my biggest fears. Saying what I want to say to take care of myself. The relationship with Naomi has taught me so much. Although it has been hard, I am grateful that I have had the sister that I have. My fear around it is gone.

2008 Big Changes

One of the new buzz words is soul mates. Supposedly a soul mate is that perfect person for you. What does that mean? Is everything supposed to be perfect? If that is the case, I am in deep trouble. To me a soul mate is there to teach you. To help you grow. If it were a perfect match and nothing went wrong, how would you grow? Ed and I still have our ups and downs. I believe this is what a soul mate relationship is all about; the ups and downs and what you learn from them.

I have never really dealt with the money issues I have and although I am earning my own money, it feels like Ed is in control. Why do I feel judged about how I spend money? Is that mine or does Ed really judge me? I have learned so much but he doesn't seem to notice.

Money is a big issue for us and always has been. Ed still thinks of me as that young girl who spent without thinking, who bought everything and anything she wanted just because. I am not that girl anymore. I am a grown woman who enjoys nice things and yet never spends more than I have. I said before that Ed has taught me a great deal about money, yet he doesn't see that I am changing and learning from what he has taught me and showed me by how he deals with money. I know this because of the snide remarks if I came home with something I have bought. He'll say, "What did you get now?" or "Oh, packages in hand." If I have something on that he hasn't seen, he says, "Is that new?" I take it as a dig but maybe it isn't, maybe it's just my perception.

One of the best things Ed has taught me is don't owe anyone anything. We are free of debt, no credit card debt. He pays everything off every month. I do the same with my own accounts. I have my own checking account and charge cards. It just makes it easier for me to have some freedom, not having to explain myself all the time about what I have spent. It seems to me he is very resentful if I ask him for anything but if something is his idea he hands money over like it is water.

Ed and I are on a walk. I say, "I want a "BONUS", some money just for me. No questions asked." He laughed and says, "You want a bonus?" A few days later, he hands me a check for $5000.00. WOW! Really? I am so excited. I am thinking of what I can do with this money. The first thing I do is put half of it in an envelope in my drawer. I will keep this for things I want in the future. I put the rest in my checking account to use for what I want. It feels like freedom for me. But it doesn't last. Ed has given me money every year for four years but he doesn't like it. He says, "This is the last check I will give you. You just spend it all and it drives me crazy." "Don't you understand what this means to me?" I say, "It is about freedom; it is about not having to ask you or anyone for money." He doesn't understand. He says "It is OUR money." I say, "I still feel I have to justify to you everything I spend and I don't like it." It doesn't matter. I don't get another check.

It feels like I have to ask permission to spend anything. We think so differently about money yet neither of us were willing to give in to the other. We are in a huge power struggle.

Our backgrounds are so different and I understand where he is coming from, being poor was no fun for sure. There were also no women in his house except his mother. He has five brothers and his dad. They never understood what it meant to have a woman in the house or what it cost. He thinks I indulge myself with makeup and lotions or for that matter whatever I buy for myself. And he tells me so. "You spend whatever you get and I don't like it," he says. I have my nails done every week. I started that after I quit biting them and he says, "That's way over the top." I say, "Too bad. I love getting my nails done." I try not to let his criticism stop me. But I feel anxious about money all the time.

But what about my fears about money? I brought those all into the marriage as well. I still felt guilty for spending anything. Instead of impulse shopping, I am careful and thoughtful about what I buy. For Ed not to notice hurts. I feel invisible. I felt it after the Cancer. I felt it when Ed became friends with other women but I don't know what to do about it.

I have just come home with a bag of something. "How much did that cost?" he says. It's not a calm voice. He's really not interested in what I have, but is sarcastic and angry. I've had enough. I'm so tired of this. "I'm sick of being treated like a child. I don't spend too much and I'm sick of being treated this way." Ed says, "You spend too much and I will never change my mind about that." I'm furious. "Your wrong and I have changed and you don't even notice. I never spend more than I have." Even though we are mad at each other, we head out to dinner at our favorite deli not saying one word all through dinner, then Ed complains about the bill. "This is too much, the wine is too expensive." We are in the car. I'm screaming at him saying, "If you think I'm expensive now, what do you think it will cost if we get divorced?" I think to myself, "When do I come first? When do you want nice things for me? When do you truly like who I am?" I don't say anything because I am so angry plus I don't think he will hear me. Our pattern is to get mad at

221

each other and not talk about it, not settle it. I stay mad for a few days pouting and being quiet and then it just stops. Ed may say something cute like, "How's it going, Les?" and I melt.

There was the affair, then Jan, then the book store fiasco. When does he choose me? The last time he chose me was when he got out of treatment and I'm not even sure that was about me. When Ed is asked about why we got back together, he always says, "I just didn't want anyone else raising my kids." I don't think he means it badly, he just doesn't hear what it sounds like. So why wouldn't I continue to think, "When do I become the one he wants to spend time with and share with? "

I sleep in the little bedroom, which is something I said I would never do. If we didn't sleep together, what did we have left? I cry all night long. Saturday afternoon while sitting in the living room, he says, "Can't we just get back to where we were?" I say, "Not this time. You won't talk about your feelings and until you do and deal with your part in this, it will not work. I will take responsibility for my part but I didn't get here alone. We never resolve this issue. We just forget about it and hope it doesn't happen again but it always does."

Ed says, "Whenever I talk about my feeling it never works out." We don't talk the rest of the evening.

The next morning he asks where the suitcases are. I tell him and he packs a bag and is preparing to leave. As he comes down the stairs he says, "I'm going to the shop for a little while and then find a place to stay." My response is "I'm sorry you feel that way. I was hoping you would fight for us." Stay and talk about what is wrong with this relationship. But he doesn't stay. He leaves. I don't know when or if he will be back.

I am thinking, when will this happen again, when will he not like me again? All of a sudden he doesn't like me. I am doing the same as

I have always done but he gets mean and nasty. I never know when it will happen and always take on that I have done something even though we don't talk about it. I shut down. "Oh, he will get over it. He will be okay in a week or so." Not this time. This is not the usual pattern for me. I usually just feel terrible and don't say anything. It kind of just came out but it felt wonderful.

I have no idea what will happen. Will he want a divorce? Will he want to come home? Yet my fear is gone. I am sitting in the living room. It is May in Minnesota and the weather is wonderful. It is sunny and bright. I am in my black leather chair that I sit in to watch television looking out to the back yard at the bird feeders we have hanging from the upper deck. We get all kinds of birds that I love but I think I like the orioles the most. They are my high school mascot. They are so beautiful and come every year to eat the grape jelly I put out.

As I sit in the chair I think about our life. This is so different for me when I left for six weeks. Whatever happens is supposed to happen and I can't try to figure it out any longer or fix it alone. I have to let it go. I am worth more than sarcasm and snide remarks. Bottom line is I can be alone if I have to be. I would rather not be but can do it if I have to.

My voice is loud and clear.

It's a week later and Ed has come over to talk. We are sitting at the kitchen table and really talking for the first time in a long time. I asked him the three things I had been thinking about.

When do I come first?

When do you want nice things for me?

When do you truly like who I am?

He starts to talk about what he wants and says:

1. Sometimes you take over in groups of friends and I don't have a chance to talk - I do

2. He says, "I don't do nice things for you because you do them
for yourself. - I do

(Because of past experiences I think if I don't do those things for
myself no one will. Beth had bought me a beautiful vase for my birthday with daisy's etched on it. Our kitchen is decorated with daisy wall
paper. She said she hoped Ed would bring me daisies once in awhile.
He doesn't.)

We have been talking for about two hours. Ed says, "I don't feel
right about the way the conversation is going." I am surprised because
I think we are getting somewhere. Something upset him and I have
no idea what it is. He leaves but about an hour later calls me and says,
"I'm going back to the hotel." I ask him to come for dinner on Monday to talk more. This is what I do, I try to fix it, but this feels different. It's the first time we have really talked out loud. Even though he
got upset, it's more than has happened in a long time.

It's Monday night and Ed is home for dinner and looks sad and
forlorn. We are talking again. It's been several more hours. He tells
me, "It's been awful at the hotel, a bad neighborhood and the police came in the middle of the night for someone. It's terrible." I say,
"Why don't you stay home." Not much is settled but it does feel right
to have him home.

Why do I love this man? He can be so infuriating but so vulnerable and so loving. He hardly remembers anything I tell him but I
know deep down he loves me or he wouldn't have come back. He just
doesn't know how to express it. I talk a lot about my fear but he also
has a great deal of fear around rejection. Maybe I love him because
of his dry sense of humor. Maybe it's because I have always thought
of him as very handsome, maybe it's because he is a good provider.
I'm not sure; does it matter? I just know I do love him. Maybe I don't
need to know anymore than that.

We are out to dinner with Beth, Steve and T.J.. I step back. I am paying attention to what Ed has said. It is not hard for me. I feel I owe Ed the respect to honor what he has asked of me. I do the same things when we are out with some new friends for dinner. I took the flowers out of the vase I keep in the kitchen and it had been empty for almost a month. Ed just walked in with daisies.

Ed and I finally sit down to talk. I say, "I want you to be present in my life, to notice me, to pay attention, to make a choice for me." He does. He starts asking me questions about what I have done during the day. He wants to know about what I am doing. Even though he thinks the healing work is really weird, he asks about it and how I feel. We are talking again, sharing things like we used to right after treatment.. We have talked about money. Ed says, "Let's try to figure out a better way of doing money together." We have a new plan. Ed will still give me a set amount of money every month but all the household bills would come out of the joint checking account. I say, "I think this way you will see what it costs to run the household." He agrees. I will still take care of my own needs as I am getting retirement from Honeywell and my Social Security. He also says, "I want to change the way I think about money." He tells me he talked to Tom, a very good friend who says, "Are you kidding? She doesn't spend hardly anything and you can pay the bills, right? So what is the big deal?" That forever changes us. I don't feel any resentment from him about money. I am also not taking advantage of the new plan but doing what I need to do for myself.

The only thing I ever wanted from Ed is the same respect he asked from me. Honor my request. Do not be snide and caustic with me. Just be honest. That is happening, but I'm not completely sure it will last. It has been so unpredictable over the years; why would it be different now? I still don't trust.

Once we get back into our routine after Ed comes home, things start to go back to the way they were before he left. But this time, I begin to notice that this is the way Ed is and start to accept that it is not about me. If it is, he can tell me otherwise, if he doesn't speak up I will let it go. He has a pattern. I'm never sure when it will happen but I am much more aware. He may come home complaining about work even though I know he loves it and then get quiet. I think, "He sees so many people all day long. All he wants is space and quiet." I can give him that.

My Excuses

It's a year later. A few of us start a new women's group and we are working on Wayne Dyer's book "Excuses Begone." I want to get a different perspective on how to think. What excuses do I have that get me into trouble? What are the things I say to myself that are not true? How do I change the thoughts in my head?

One of the things Dyer says that has stuck with me is, "When you change the way you look at things, the things you look at change." I just love that and I'm saying it over and over all day long.

I am changing the way I think and look about Ed. He is a good man. We all have our defenses. If I can let go of mine, I can be honest and let go of the fear of being who I am with everyone, not just my family. As I said before I am noticing things more. Instead of always thinking his mood is about me, that I must have done something, I don't react to it. I use my intuition to guide what I should do. If I ask questions and try to figure out what is wrong with him, it only makes it worse so I just wait it out. If it gets to a point of being really uncomfortable, I may say something like, "Whats up?" Sometimes this works and we have great conversations and sometimes it doesn't. But I'm OK.

If I can look at fear as a way of growing I can change how I look at FEAR! Maybe that is what I'm supposed to learn from all the fear I have carried all my life. Look past the fear. A little book I read years ago was called "Feel the Fear and Do it Anyway" I am learning to do that more and more every day. There are things I will always carry with me from my past. If I am not afraid of them I will learn to accept them and love myself anyway. Fear of Money, Fear of being fat, fear of not being liked. Maybe these are issues I will have all my life I don't know I only know I am working on them.

Australia

Ever since I read the book "The Thorn Birds," I have wanted to go to Australia. Kathy and I have talked about going in a year. Ed and I are on a walk and I say, "Kathy and I are talking about going to Australia next year." He says, "Why are you waiting a year? Why not go now?" Now isn't that sweet?

Kathy and I are going for three weeks with a tour group. We were supposed to leave October 29th, 2011. It's early on the morning we are to leave. I get a call saying, "Don't go to the airport. Qantas may be going on strike." They did. We are not able to reschedule until January 2012.

Its January 7th, 2012, we are at the airport ready to leave Minneapolis for Australia. After a long flight and a couple plan changes, we are in Cairns, I don't feel jet lagged but everyone says, "It's because even though you have been traveling for twenty-four hours it is the same time as home, just a different day."

What an amazing trip! We are heading to the Great Barrier Reef to snorkel. I have never seen such blue water. We visit the aboriginal spiritual rock, Uluru. Such an amazing place. We have an outback dinner and learn so many things about this country. It is vast. One person for every two hundred miles.

I had not realized I was afraid of heights until a previous trip I took with the girls to Mexico. We went to some ruins and I climbed up to the top. When I turned around I realized with a shock that I couldn't get down. Each one of my friends took turns sitting with me as I went down one step at a time on my butt. After that my stomach would roll every time I was up too high. I started sitting on the aisle seat on an airplane because I couldn't stand to see the ground go away.

When we arrived in Sydney, our tour guide asked if anyone wanted to climb the Sydney Bridge. Kathy and I both say, "Yes." Oh boy, what have I done? Can I overcome my fear of heights? Can I face the fear head on? I climb that bridge, all one thousand three hundred and ninety steps.

We are connected to the bridge with a metal slider that goes all the way up and down. It gets pretty windy up here so even our hat and glasses are hooked on to us. We have on one piece suits. Six of us from our group are climbing. Everyone knows I am doing this to overcome a fear of heights. There is a walkway underneath the bridge that people can walk over the lake and not have to climb. All of a sudden we hear, "Hello up there." The rest of our group is walking across underneath us and recognized us. They all yell up at me, "Good going Yeah for you!" I don't look down; I just wave and smile. I am doing it. I am already feeling so triumphant. Laughing, smiling so big I can hardly talk. I am so proud of myself and I'm not even done yet. We are coming to the top of the bridge the view is spectacular. I can see the Sydney Opera house across the bay as I look around. It is amazing. I feel no tightness in my stomach, just joy.

We are heading to New Zealand and decided to go on a jet boat ride. To get to the river, we have to take a rickety old bus up a narrow road with cliffs. We are right on the edge. I am sitting by the window and I'm not afraid. My stomach is calm. No fluttering again. I can't stop smiling. Kathy keeps asking, "Are you OK?" "Absolutely!" My fear is gone from my body at last. I know this is what the trip is for, letting go of fear.

Trying New Things, Again

After my trip, I start doing a lot of energy work. Network Spinal Analysis (NSA) is a form of chiropractic work but with energy, not adjustments. Whenever I went to a chiropractor I would tense up because I knew it would hurt. So it just wasn't working. NSA is a process of releasing all energy in your body that isn't needed. It is soft and a very light touch. It helps straighten your spine so your body feels much better. Because this type of chiropractic work believes that emotions are caught in our bodies and can cause the pain, the emotions are released. Although it is releasing emotions, you don't have to go back and figure out where the emotion comes from; you can just let it go. Feel it but let it go.

I had been having ringing in my ears for quite a while. Before I went to Australia I was very concerned about the ringing and the long flight. The NSA wasn't helping. A friend told me about a Qi Gong practitioner (Qi Gong is a Chinese healing technique) that she had been seeing. I start seeing Deanne and stopped the NSA. She has given me exercises to do at home. I keep this practice up for awhile until I realize Deanne wants me to do forty minutes of exercises a day and I just don't know how to fit it in. I am back to NSA and feel wonderful.

My niece Sandy introduces me to Laurie, who does intuitive readings. Ed calls this really woo-woo stuff. She channels angels and others that have passed on. I am meeting with her the first time. She tells me my parents are with me and want no one else to be with me for the half hour because they want me to know how proud they are of me and who I have become. I am in tears.

I ask them about Naomi whether there is anything else I can do about our relationship? They say, "NO! Let it go."

Anita is asking permission from my parents to come talk to me. It is amazing. I have missed her so much that knowing she is with me is wonderful.

I am sitting with Laurie again and my mother comes in to talk to me. I apologize to my mother, "Mom, I am so sorry for getting mad at you when I was sixteen. I didn't know what else to do." She says, "I never knew what it was all about. I never knew why you were so mad." I tell her about the fight I overheard, and say, "I didn't realize then that I was afraid to get mad at Dad but somewhere deep down, I knew no matter what I did, you would always love me." It is one of the best and freeing experiences I have had. I know she is here and we are sharing a special moment. Forgiveness. I believe all things are possible, so when Laurie tells me my parents and Anita are with me I know they are.

Because of my newfound strength, I am able to work on the committee for our 50th high school class reunion. Since I hated high school I wasn't sure how this would be. I start to connect with women I haven't seen for a very long time. It is amazing how many of the people I thought were having a wonderful time in school hated it. I was not as alone as I thought. The actual reunion was the most fun I think I have had in years. We laughed, danced and literally were drunk on happiness. Life is taking a new path. Not only am I letting go of old fears I am feeling good about myself

Ed and I are standing at the sink washing dishes; we wash dishes every night together. I wash, he dries. I only use the dishwasher when we have company. I like the time together. We are watching Wheel of Fortune and guessing what the sayings are going to be. We are a little competitive because we both like to win, but are laughing. All of a sudden he says, "I have been thinking about something but haven't said it. You have a lot of courage." I don't know what to say, so I don't say anything. After thinking about it for a very short time I say, "I'm sorry I didn't respond and thank you. What a wonderful thing to say to me." I also ask him, "Why do you feel that way?" he says, "Because you are always trying new things. You never give up and that takes courage." I had never thought of it that way before.

T.J.'s Bar Mitzvah

When things get unsettled for Ed and me, I remember T.J.'s Bar Mitzvah.

T.J. is being raised Jewish, and at thirteen he had a Bar Mitzvah. This is a celebration to become an adult in the synagogue.

T.J. is up on the altar and doing a beautiful job reciting all the prayers and readings from the Torah. It is time for him to thank everyone. He thanks his grandpa Ed and starts to cry.

I remember the first time Ed held T.J. There was a light in his eyes that I had not seen before. When his own kids were little, he hardly held them. He was afraid of them until they were able to walk. Not this little boy. He held him for hours. He played with him on the floor as he did with our kids but he could tell T.J. he loved him and be vulnerable with him. Their relationship is mutual. T.J. adores his grandpa and the same light fills his eyes when he looks at Ed. There is a trust between them that was just there from the day he was born.

Beth whispers to me, "I think maybe this is the first time T.J. really realizes what a unique and wonderful relationship he has with his grandpa." We are all crying at this point including Ed. The rabbi is terrific. He has taken T.J. over to the side and helps him calm down. It takes a few tense minutes to see if he can recover. He does and comes back to finish the ceremony like a true pro. Ed said after it was all over, "The Jewish religion is so welcoming. I felt included in the ceremony even though I am Catholic." Steve and T.J.'s synagogue is a very open synagogue very different from the one that I had gone to with Beth and Steve years before. They accept everyone. It is the kind of synagogue my parents would have belonged to if they had felt they wanted to go. I did see the same light in Ed's eyes when he held Sam for the first time but we don't see him enough so the bond is not quite the same.

A New Way of Behaving

I have learned that God, or the Universe as I call it, is within all of us, never wanting anything but the best for us. If we can listen to our inner feeling, we can have whatever we want. When we are kind, sincere, honest and most of all loving, all things will be. I know this is what my parents tried to teach me. Although it has taken a long time to understand, I finally get it. Be the kind of people they were and wanted us to be. Live with all people no matter their color or political beliefs. Also have love for all people. And forgive.

I am sitting at my computer checking emails when I see Naomi's name come up. My heart starts to pound, and I think "Oh No, what have I done now?" A couple weeks ago she sent me two really nasty emails about something she thought I had done wrong.

I open this email because although I always delete them now without answering I always read them. This starts out a little differently. "Leslie, is there any way we can find a way to work on our relationship and forgive each other?"

I am absolutely stunned. Although I have told her several times before, I answer with, "I am more than willing to talk about our relationship but I won't do it over email. If you want to get together or come over just give me a call." An hour later the phone rings. We talk for a few seconds and decide to have lunch the following Monday. I am sitting at the table at the deli that we like, and she walks in and sits down. We chit chat for almost forty-five minutes, and then I run out of things to say. I start thinking to myself, "I'm not leaving here today without settling some of this stuff." I say, "Did you want to talk about our relationship?" She says, "Yes, do you have an expectation?" "Naomi," I say, "I have no expectations and I have forgiven you a long time ago for any perceived hurts." I'm not sure where that came from but it was perfect because it took away blame. "But I am frustrated." "Why?" she asks."

The nasty emails have to stop. When I see your name come up on the screen, my hands get all sweaty and I get nervous wondering what is going to come at me. What I want is if you hear anything I have said or anything I have done please call me and ask me my side of it.""That's reasonable," she says.

Then for the first time in my life she says, "I was a very angry child and I took it out on you. I also was very angry at our parents, but I'm not angry any longer."

I almost fall off my chair. I am so stunned I don't remember what I said.

The next day at my computer, I get an email from Naomi and in the subject line is "Positive email." What a difference a simple conversation can make.

New Conversation

I am taking a deep breath and letting it out. Ed and I are having the most wonderful conversation as we are driving to Rochester.

Before leaving we had one of our typical fights, I was giving advice and he was not listening. "Yesterday you almost tripped on the stairs. Are you worried about falling?" I asked. He had a knee replacement last October and is still not 100%. "Only in these shoes," he says.

"Why don't you go see the Medical Massage person that Pat had recommended?" Pat has had both knees replaced and really likes this woman. "No," he says. He is frustrated because nothing seems to help. "I sure would hate to have to sell this house because you aren't taking care of your knee." That's when he gets mad. "I'm fine," he says, but I know he isn't. For some reason I start laughing because it is so common of him to disregard what I say. I am beginning to respond to this with humor rather than anger, which makes him even madder.

On the way to Rochester, I am wondering if I can say what I am thinking. The tension is killing me and I want this to be a fun day. I take the risk. "You know sometimes I know things. Sometimes I know what I am talking about more than you do. You know many, many things but sometimes I know also. Why is your first response either a no or getting mad at me?"

He kind of sighs. "I think men are taught that we are the providers that we have to know everything and be on top of everything. We are supposed to take care of our families and know what is best," he says.

As he is talking his truth to me, I see what he means. "It's OK with me if you are not right all the time," I say. "I get it. I understand where this is all coming from and I agree with you. But let's change this. Let's acknowledge what the other one knows. I know more about the physical body then you do. I have so much knowledge about how it works and how to take care of it. You have knowledge about so many other things in our lives. You take care of finances, you work hard, you pay for everything and I respect that so much. I just want you to respect and acknowledge what I know."

It's a week later. We are out walking and he is still limping. I say, "Since you are so busy at work, can I call the massage therapist for you to set it up?" I'm in his business again. Right where I shouldn't be. He hems and haws and I give a really big sign. He puts his hand on my shoulder and says, "Don't worry, Les. I'll go see her, how about this Friday?"

What a difference a day or a week makes. He just got home after his first session with her. He says, "She really worked on me. It took ninety minutes. I think I feel a little better. I signed up for ten sessions."

"Good for you. Let's hope it works." And I left it at that.

50 Years! How Can That Be?

50 Years! Ed and Me

We are at Bunny's, one of our favorite restaurants, with Beth and Steve. Beth is saying to Ed, "Where do you want to have your 50th anniversary party?" He replies, "I don't want a big party." She is getting upset. "Of course you have to celebrate. It's a big deal," I just keep quiet. We are driving home. Ed puts his arm around me and says, "You know I love ya Les. I just don't like big parties." "I know," I reply," I understand."

Because I know how Ed feels about parties I have started planning my own 70th birthday party. I love big parties. I decide to have a luncheon with all the women that have been important to me in my life.

I reserve the patio room at Eden Avenue Grill, another favorite restaurant, and invite thirty-five women. Thirty women respond "Yes." I am surprised by this. Beth is helping plan every detail, everything from the name tags, to little gift bags. The bags will be filled with retro candy, bubble gum cigarettes, wax lips, jacks, button candy, nut goodies and salted nut rolls. I am seating women who don't know each other next to each other.

Beth and I are shopping for bags and tissue. She insists on a deep yellow and bright pink, the same as the name tags. Not my favorite. I like canary yellow and light pink but she is very insistent, so I give in. It's OK

Sandy and Beth and I are at my house putting bags together. We are all laughing and having such a good time. I am getting very excited about my party. The invitation says, "Put on your best dress and join me for lunch." I want to have a lunch that has lots of memories for me. Mom and Grandma used to take us downtown to Dayton's for lunch at the Skyroom and I always had creamed chicken on a patty shell. Mom also got me a doll cake for several birthdays. The restaurant is making the creamed chicken for me and Byerly's has doll cakes.

Beth and I are at the restaurant meeting with the owners and the women who will manage the party. Beth has such good ideas and we are all laughing and kidding around. We are deciding on how to put the table in the new patio room that has a retractable roof. It's sunny and bright. It also has a fireplace if it's cold. What I didn't know was Beth was planning her own surprise.

On Thursday night, I made dinner for the family. Greg and Sam have come from California to celebrate with us. I am so glad they are here. We don't get much time with Sam. It's also T.J.'s eighteenth birthday; his birthday is the day after mine.

We are heading down to the living room and Beth is setting up the computer. I wonder what she is doing. Then she starts the video she has made of my life. It is amazing. She has captured so many good things. I am on the verge of tears.

It's Saturday morning and I'm on my way to get the doll cake and go to the restaurant to help get everything ready. I'm all dressed up and feel wonderful. I walk into the patio room and it's at least ninety degrees in the room its then I realize there is no air conditioning. OH WELL! What am I going to do? Go somewhere else? I am putting the bags on the tables and in walks Sandy. She has this cute t-shirt on. It says, "Les is More, Happy 70th." As each of the women come in they have on the same Tee. Beth had them made and ordered one for each woman. Kathy tells me that Beth was absolutely sure I would be angry because I wanted a dress up party, but I am so overwhelmed and delighted I can't put words to it.

Everyone is given a glass of champagne as they walk in and wine is served throughout lunch. I have written a little speech that will be hard for me to read but very important for me to say. Here it is:

You have all been invited to help me celebrate my 70th birthday because you have all had an impact on my life and have helped me become the person I am today. This party is not only to celebrate my birthday but to celebrate and honor you.

It is kind of like the book Anne Freeman's Fabulous Traveling Funeral *although not a funeral thank goodness. It is about bringing important people in my life together. If you haven't read it, do. It's wonderful.*

Some of you I have known my whole life. My sister Naomi, my cousin Roxanne. Others I have known their whole lives. Beth and my niece Sandy.

Some of you are longtime friends although I think Judy is the longest like sixty years and some short like Penny, Karen and Pat. But no more or less important. I have known you all in different aspects of my life. Some work, some travel, some golf. I have known you all different lengths of time but you have all had an impact.

Roz, I look up to you as someone I hope to be at 90 and a cougar no less. You show me how to be in this world, loving, kind and gracious.

Reva, thank you so much for doing the flowers. My heart sings.

All of you have helped me grow, some spiritually, or as Ed would say my woo-woo friends, some I travel with and golf with. I'm not sure how much I've grown in the golf department but we do have fun. Some I have worked with at all the many jobs and all of you just teaching me how to live every day to the fullest.

Beth, there aren't enough words that can express how I feel about what you have done for me. So for now Thank You will have to do, you are an amazing women and I love you.

You have all been in my life for a reason and I am grateful. You are wonderful friends and I thank you. Now let's have fun meet and talk to those you don't know and celebrate.

Reading this out loud to all my friends reminded me of where I have come from and how much I have grown. I HAVE A VOICE.

You may have noticed that I mentioned my sister. I had invited her because I wanted bygones to be bygones. She came up to me at the party and asked if we could do another lunch.

"I have bought you a little gift but didn't bring it today because you said no gifts," she says. "Sure. Let's find a day that works," I say.

We are at breakfast. The gift she has brought me was very special and very much about who I am. It is called "The Student." She also gives me a card with a typed note inside.

"Read it when you get home," she says. We part on a happy note and say let's do this again soon. I get home and open up the note. It is the first apology my sister has ever made to me. She says, "I can't imagine the terror you must have felt when those dogs were charging at you." What a wonderful way to end a wonderful celebration: a new and different relationship with my only sister.

Ed was amazed at the note when I showed him and just smiled that sweet smile of his.

CONCLUSION

How I feel about politics and its role in my life today:

In November 2010, I was able to connect with Alan Larkin, the son of artist and teacher Eugene Larkin. We talked about the McCarthy era and how it affected others who knew my parents. I was hoping it would help me understand why this has played such a big role in my life.

Alan was very open with me and willing to share his thoughts about this time. He tells me his mother had vivid recollections that were very painful. "She has passed away," Alan says, "but, she would have loved to talk to you about them." Alan suggests that we set a day for me to call Gene and he will be there to interpret for us. Gene is in a nursing home and has some dementia. His memory is clouded so the information is not really clear. I am able to have a short conversation with him .

Gene tells me, "On one day I got a phone call from the FBI, they wanted to talk. This was the first he knew about any of this, the next thing he knew they were at his door." They picked him up and drove him around. Asking him to name names of people who were Communists. If he didn't tell them, he would end up in jail. They were very rough with him. He said he was very afraid. At that time, he lived in Kansas and worked in Pittsburgh. There were open coalmines and people would drop out of sight. There was a lot of fear. After that they would just park outside his home and wait for him to do something. He lost a teaching position over the accusations. His dean said if he resigned he would not get fired. That is when he came to Minneapolis. Where he became friends with my family. The FBI followed him here. He never went to jail.

Just one month after I spoke with him, Gene passed away. Another voice from that era has been stilled. Alan also said he and his brother are very active in politics. Their fear is not the same as mine.

Lionel Davis is another person I talked to. He was a friend of my grandparents although my parents age. He told me pretty much the same story I had been hearing from others. How afraid they were. How the FBI followed them around. In 1951 a front page story in the newspaper accused Lionel of being Communist. He had a hard time getting a job after that. He decided he was not cut out to be a political organizer and backed off. His children are not involved in politics at all, although he said they did turn to religion.

I also spent a few hours with Ellen, the daughter of Dad's best friend. We grew up together and our families were very close. She told me she always respected her father because he handled his business success without compromising his political principles. He was a chemist and worked for General Mills. Later he had his own company. He was about to lose his largest account because he had refused to sign a loyalty oath and signing was a condition for continuation of the working relationship. A loyalty oath is an oath of loyalty to an organization, institution, or state of which an individual is a member. This being the United States. Many who, were accused of being communist were asked to sign this oath. Mike did not sign it and left General Mills.

Ellen said she has not taken the steps to get her FBI files even though she is sure she has one. In the 1950 and 60's those on the "left" were followed with near paranoid interest by the FBI, Because she was involved as a teenager and beyond into the Vietnam era, she is sure they knew about her.

Ellen said, "I remember going around the neighborhood as a young kid with a wagon and literature about the Rosenbergs. I was passionately interested in this case and so opposed to the entire idea of the electric chair for people whose case was not concretely proven." At age twelve I read the Rosenberg's "Death House Letters" that they wrote to each other while awaiting execution. I cried,"

At age twelve, I had no idea who the Rosenbergs were or what the "Death House Letters" were. The Rosenberg's were accused of being spies for Russia at the start of the Korean war in 1951. They were imprisoned and because they could not afford bail they were in prison the last three years of their life. The "Death House Letters" are letters they wrote to each other during the three years they were there. They were found guilty in a civil trial and executed as spies in 1953. This was also going on at the same time my family was being accused of being communist. Years later it was proven they were innocent.

Ellen told me her family had many open conversations about politics in front of the children, while my family was secretive. There was so much whispering or talking in Yiddish so we wouldn't understand. Though I now understand they thought they were protecting us, it just became another fear.

While reading my grandparents FBI files I saw a story about a movie called "Salt of the Earth." they labeled it subversive. I decided to rent it to see what they considered subversive. It was a story about the Mexican American coal miners in New Mexico in the 50's. They were treated very badly and went on strike for better benefits. Simple things like running water in their homes.

What I found most interesting is that the husbands treated their wives like the owners of the mines treated them. They just didn't count. They wouldn't listen to them or let them help. The women were to stay home and take care of the house and children. Nothing else. Finally the women stood up for themselves and took over the pick-it line to help the men. They did get some improvements, but not many. What is subversive about that story? It was the times. It was real. It had happened.

I am more politically aware than I ever have been. I don't read much about it, although I have strong opinions. Today seems to me so much like the McCarthy era. People judging others for who they are if their beliefs are different from their own. Don't we learn from our mistakes? Will we continue on this path of destruction? Can we learn a different way? I hope so. Surprisingly Ed and I believe the same things politically. We watch Bill Maher every Friday night. Other than voting, this is about as much politics as I can handle. I don't like to argue over politics. I think it is useless to try to convince others to believe the same way I do. I feel the same about religion.

How are my money issues?

I still obsess about money. I have just come back from seeing Pat Kaluza, an astrologer, I have seen several times over the last few years. She says, "Maybe this money issue isn't yours. Maybe you are carry-ing around your parents ideas about money and need to start figuring out your own beliefs around money." I do love my new mantra about money, "Money always works out." and it does. Letting go of the ob-session is the next step for me and I know I'll get there. She also says, "You have been on a journey for thirty years to find out who you are. You have come to the end of that journey. Now it is time to live what you have learned." Ed and I don't fight about money anymore. He is generous and kind. Even though I know he doesn't understand what I do with money, he leaves it up to me, most of the time. This is my issue to understand and I'm working on it.

Weight – Will I ever Let go of it?

Today I am 118 pounds. I wear between a size two and six. Do I still feel fat? Sometimes. Do I think Ed will leave or not like me if I get fat? NO! I want to keep my weight down for me. I like how I feel at this weight. I still watch everything I eat but not obsessively. Last night I had a small hot fudge sundae as a treat; it was delicious.

Naomi and Phyllis

It has been well over a year and I have not had one single nasty email from Naomi. It feels really good to have her name come up on my computer and not be afraid. We are able to be together and have breakfast or lunch and are getting along very well. It makes me happy.

Phyllis and I have not spoken for many many years. Sometimes I miss her. I am not sure what I will do about it but it is something I will think about and decide.

Do I invite people back into my life that have hurt me? It is a question I will need to answer. When I spoke to a friend about this she said, it is not your job to make this relationship right. I think I agree. Yet, it still makes me sad.

Ed and I

Ed and I are doing really well. It's hard for us both to believe we have been married 50 years. He still doesn't get who I am all the time but you know sometimes I don't get who he is and it's fine. We laugh and have fun together.

Its 7:30 am, we are sitting at the kitchen table having coffee and reading the paper. T.J.just called, "Do you guys want to go out to breakfast?" Ed's not sure he wants to rush out but I say, "Sure. When and where?" He's off to college in August so we won't have the opportunity much longer.

We are sitting at the table in Perkins and talking. Ed gives me what I used to call the DUMB SHIT look. I say to T.J., "See that look? That is what I call the dumb shit look. It used to put me in tears. Not anymore." Ed says something else and T.J.starts to laugh. Ed says, "What's so funny?" "You are trying so hard not to give Grandma that look again," T.J. says. We all burst out laughing.

The old fear is gone. I do not think fear ever goes away completely. I have worked so hard on becoming the person I want to be. Even though I know I will never end my search for who I am, I am more comfortable than ever with who I am now. This helps in all my relationships. Especially the one with Ed. Acceptance: that's what it's all about. Acceptance of each other for who we are, not who we want each other to be.

Some friends have come and gone in my life but now I take responsibility in my relationships. In return, I hope the loyalty and trust that I offer will come back to me. It surely did at my party. Feeling betrayed has been a constant theme throughout my life. I recognize this now as a personal lesson. I am learning everyday to think before I speak. When it is fear that holds me back I try and look at the cause and ask why do I have it? Can I do this anyway? Whatever it is? Sometimes it is not fear. Sometimes it is learning to accept people as they are and allow them to be different.

My life is driven by spirituality, not religion. In refection, this is the gift my family gave to me.

I have a sign on my refrigerator from my niece Sandy. She made it when Jim died.

"Peace"
It does not mean to be in a place where there is no noise, trouble or hard work.
It means to be in the midst of those things and
still be calm in your heart."

I look at my life with Ed as a gift now. All the stress, all the experiences have been a learning process for me. What an amazing ride it's been. And will continue to be!

Our Family Today

Greg and Beth took this for Ed's 50th birthday

Some things stay the same

T.J.

Sam

Permissions

Books written by Joan Borysenko

Mending the body Minding the Mind

Guilt is the Teacher, Love is the Lesson

Fire in the Soul

Pocketful of Miracles

The Power of the Mind to Heal

A Women's Book of Life

The Ways of the Mystic

A Women's Journey to God

Inner Peace for Busy People

Inner Peace for Busy Women

The Hoffman Process By Joan B. and Tim Lawrence

7 Paths to God

Your Souls Compass, What us Spiritual Guidance

CPSIA information can be obtained at www.ICGtesting.com
Printed in the USA
VOW07s0119061115

51299LV00021B/63/P